WICCA FOR BEGINNERS

Guide to Learn the Secrets of Witchcraft with Wiccan Spells, Moon Rituals, Tarot, Meditation, Herbal Power, Crystal, and Candle Magic (2022 Crash Course for Newbies)

Otis Elledge

CONTENTS

INTRODUCTION

Welcome to the vast world of Wicca, a collection of beliefs, rituals, and traditions that have spread throughout the Western world since the mid-twentieth century. Immerse yourself in a belief system that reintroduces us to nature and the spiritual realm, all while practising self-care and personal empowerment. We are all inextricably linked—to one another, to the earth and the physical realm, and to the spiritual energy that pervades the universe.

Utilize this knowledge to create a life of purpose and fulfilment.

To begin comprehending what Wicca is and what the religion can mean to you, it is necessary to first comprehend what Wicca is not. This is critical because there is a great deal of misinformation about Wicca in the world. To maintain your relationship with nature during your journey into Wicca, it is critical to separate the white noise from the truth of Wicca.

Wicca is not a religious cult. This is a critical point to grasp if you wish to have a Wiccan relationship with the world. Additionally, practising witchcraft does not imply membership in a cult.

In essence, becoming a Wiccan entails holding all life in high regard.

Given that Wiccans can and do practise spell magic, this is essentially what this book will be about. The primary objective of this book is to familiarise you with basic spells and magic that you can use in your daily life as a Wiccan witch. There are spells that are intended for covens to perform, but for the purposes of this guide, I will omit them.

I'll concentrate on the wonders that you, as an individual, can accomplish. If you're still navigating the Wicca religion and honing your spellcasting skills, this book is exactly what you've been looking for.

To be a Wiccan does not require membership in a coven. Numerous Wiccans practise their religion and magic independently. This is the focus of this guide—your individual journey into the world of Wicca and witchcraft.

Wicca is an incredible journey that strengthens your connection to the world, but, like any religion, it is founded on certain fundamental principles and rules.

Wicca is fundamentally an inclusive belief system that places a premium on our interactions with the natural and spiritual realms. Anyone wishing to channel their energy into a positive and powerful life of intention and accomplishment can begin today by practising Wicca!

Chapter 1
Introduction to Wicca

Wicca is a way of life that is frequently referred to as a religion. It establishes the foundation for people to live and work in harmony with their environment.

When you live the Wiccan way, you live in a way that promotes community with the godly and with everything created by the Divine.

By choosing the Wiccan path, you agree to live in profound awe and appreciation of the natural world. You are expressing gratitude for the world in which you live, from the sunrise and sunset to the growing and harvesting of plants and the natural lifecycles of the animals in your vicinity. Everything that is a part of your natural world becomes sacred to you when you view it as a sacred gift from the world.

This pre-Christian belief system originated in Ireland, Scotland, and Wales. There, our forefathers and mothers learned how to coexist in harmony with the natural world, honouring the

Divine in all things and cherishing all that was. Much of the information used in modern Wicca comes from these ancient traditions, though the tradition has incorporated a great deal of modern information and twists since then.

It is critical to understand that Wicca encompasses a variety of "types" of belief systems. Numerous offshoots of the original traditions have developed, allowing for the incorporation of a wide variety of belief systems into their way of life. This way, regardless of your beliefs, you are likely to find someone in the Wiccan faith who shares them, allowing you to connect with others who can assist you in developing your own practises and learning more about yourself and this complex belief system.

We are merely a part of the Earth, no more or less than any other crawling, flying, or swimming creature. As such, it is our responsibility to care for, heal, and protect all living things. To be a Wiccan is to give selflessly, to assume the role of a teacher, and to be constantly on the lookout for ways to improve.

To be a Wiccan is to recognise the power inherent in everything and every creature. As a Wiccan, it is up to you to recognise divine power in whatever form it chooses to take. This face may take the form of naked tree branches shivering in the autumn wind or the promise contained within each petal of a budding flower in spring.

The mediaeval church made a concerted effort to demonise the Wiccan religion. However, being Wiccan entails becoming a promoter of peace and setting an example through a nonviolent lifestyle. Our objective is to coexist peacefully with all other creatures on this planet and with the divine powers that surround us.

As a Wiccan, it is critical for you to understand that we reject the concept of absolute evil such as Satan. Unlike other religions' adherents, Wiccans are not motivated by fear of "afterlife punishment" or "eternal damnation." Rather than that, Wiccans are encouraged to be kind to others and to "behave" appropriately in this life.

Another long-standing misconception is that Wicca is a cult.

Increasing our numbers and manipulating people's minds in order to gain power has never been a Wiccan way of doing things. On the contrary, being a Wiccan entails accepting diversity. As Wiccans, we always respect and uphold the individual's right to live his or her life however he or she wishes.

Does this mean that the Wiccan faith is devoid of rules?

Wicca as a religion follows a set of fundamental rules. The first of these principles is the Wiccan Rede, which states that as long as no one is harmed, one may do as one pleases. Wiccans are discouraged from using magic to intentionally harm another living being as a result of this rule.

Being Wiccan entails being in tune with the universe. As a result, you'll be able to tap into the infinite reservoir of universal wisdom and gain access to magical knowledge. This privilege comes with a great deal of responsibility. As a Wiccan, you are encouraged to use magic solely for the benefit of others.

According to the Law of Threefold Return, any energy you send into the world, whether positive or negative, will return to you threefold stronger. It is critical to note that this rule is not intended to reassure obedience through fear. The universe has no intention of punishing anyone. This is a perfectly natural response. Consider the universe to be a vast ocean of energy that connects and encompasses the unique energies of all living things, including you.

When you send out ripples of energy, whether through an action or an intention, they are absorbed by that vast ocean and affect everything and everyone. However, similar to ocean waves, that energy will eventually return to touch you.

In the 1970's, there was an increase in the number of horrific criminal acts committed by members of satanic cults. Regrettably, the media incorrectly associated these activities with Wiccans, and this misunderstanding spread throughout the public. Sensing the danger, the Council of Witches established the 13 Wiccan Belief Principles to govern Wiccan practise.

Until today, a sizable number of covens have created mandates using this model. The central tenet of these principles is that we are obligated to care for nature in the same way that we are obligated to allow nature to care for us.

Within each of us is an innate power that we must harness and harness in order to live in harmony with nature and all beings.

Each of us has internal and external dimensions, internal and external realities, and it is our responsibility to nurture both. As a Wiccan, you must recognise the universe's creative power, which is revealed when masculine and feminine energies converge. To Wiccans, sex is a symbol of life and a source of energy that, when used in magic, can be quite potent.

Additionally, it is necessary to keep in mind that different covens operate under distinct rules established by their respective committees. These rules are intended to assist you in making prudent use of magic. The High Priestess or High Priest of each coven is in charge. To join a coven, one must agree to live by these rules.

Additionally, you can choose to become a solitary practitioner.

Whichever path you take, keep in mind that the goodness in your heart, your conscience, and the purity of your intention serve as a far more reliable guide than any set of rigid rules.

What Exactly Is Magic?

Magical belief is an integral part of the Wiccan religion. In the simplest terms, magic is the process of harnessing the energy of the universe in order to effect change. Everything in this universe is energy-based. You are composed entirely of energy. And all of our energies are connected through what is referred to as the Universal Energy, which flows freely and indefinitely around us. Everyone was born with the ability to access and manipulate these energies in order to achieve a desired effect.

As a Wiccan, you must believe that it is your birthright to have access to this limitless source of energy in order to improve your own and others' lives. Accessing and utilising this energy is accomplished through magic and spellcasting. When you cast a spell, you are borrowing energy from the universe's divine essence. You can see now why spellcasting should be regarded as a sacred act that should not be taken lightly. It is not your responsibility to abuse the universe's powers. Wiccan practitioners use magic for meaningful purposes such as assisting a friend in recovering from illness or grief, attracting love for others or for oneself, healing the Earth, or inviting happiness into one's life.

Wicca The Fundamental Beliefs and Philosophies

Wicca can be described as a broad religion because it embraces a diverse range of perspectives, realities, and beliefs. There are, however, several major core beliefs that the majority of Wiccans adhere to in order to provide a solid foundation for comprehending the magic with which they practise.

These concepts are considered regardless of which coven you belong to or which deity you worship. The concepts discussed in this chapter serve as the primary platform, or foundation, for understanding what Wicca is and how it explains itself to those interested in following this path.

Nature is a Divine Being

The overwhelming majority of Wiccans will affirm that nature is divine. It serves as the foundation for the entire practise, and there are numerous ways in which this fundamental belief manifests itself in these rituals. Each rock, tree, leaf, plant, animal, bird, insect, and person is a member of this Earth, as are hundreds of thousands of other species and landscapes.

Our sacred home is the Earth, and we are a sacred part of it. It is the repository and generator of all life energy, and we are a part of those cycles and systems. Worshiping nature is tantamount to worshipping the essence of all things. Additionally, you will discover that all Wiccan holidays and festivals are derived from a reverence for nature.

Each festival is timed to coincide with the solstice or equinox. All esbats are determined by the lunar cycle. And nearly every ingredient in the rituals and spells associated with these celebrations is derived from nature in some way.

In nature, there is also a celebration of the cohesion of opposing forces.

There is always a balance of light and darkness, and natureworship enables us to view life from that place of equilibrium and serenity. It is the male and female presence in all things; the yin and yang. That is the way nature is.

The practise of devoting space and love to nature is a part of the Wiccan creed, and while it is not required, it comes naturally when all of the other core beliefs are considered.

Numerous tools for rituals and spells are derived from nature. You'll find yourself collecting herbs or scraps of wood to construct a wand. You may be gathering specific plants to decorate your home for a particular holiday, or you may be dressing your altar in the perfumes and trinkets of the forest floor. Wicca incorporates all of nature, and it is a highly effective method for fully connecting with the divine in nature.

Karma, Reincarnation, and the Afterlife

Karma is an echo of the Threefold Law (described below), which essentially states that what you do in this life will carry over into the next. To make such a suggestion, one must believe in reincarnation, which creates an opening for your spiritual being and essence to return to another life following your previous one in order to continue learning lessons and acquiring knowledge for the evolution of all things.

According to Wicca, this is what will always be and has always been, and so in order to embrace Wicca's principles, you must examine the reality of who you were previously and who you will become in the future. Perhaps you are already familiar with some of your previous life experiences and are aware of the lessons you are attempting to learn from them. In some cases, you acquire new knowledge along the way and are not always aware of what you are supposed to be learning. Karma requires that you remember what you need to heal from previous lives in order to ascend further into your true power and magic. And while you're at it, make certain that whatever you do in this life is something you want to carry forward into the next.

While there is a concept of reincarnation, there is also a concept of the afterlife, which is sometimes referred to as Summerland, and it is here that you rest between lives to gather your strength and reflect on the previous one in order to create the best journey forward.

All of these concepts assist the Wiccan in bridging the divide between Earth and Spirit and in understanding that the divine balance is always present, regardless of the life you are living or the stage of travel between worlds you are in.

Ancestors

It is not uncommon for Wiccan rituals and casting to invoke the ancestors. Many Wiccans believe that our ancestors are always with us, guiding us and pointing us in the right direction, and that they should be honoured for their own commitment to forging ahead and living life.

Wiccans worship a variety of deities, and it is natural to incorporate your ancestors into your practise on a similar frequency, as they are a part of the cycle of the self and have a wealth of lessons to impart as you mature and honour your own path. The concept of ancestral honour is not unique to Wicca; it is a universal truth found in the majority of religious practises.

Much of the reverence for the ancestors stems from a desire to embrace both the past and what your ancestors continue to do for you in the future.

The Year's Wheel

Wicca honours all of the year's cycles. Every solstice, as well as every equinox, has a celebration, or Sabbat. The rituals and spells associated with these times are a sacred commemoration and celebration of the end of something in order to herald the beginning of something new. There are an infinite number of deaths and rebirths on the calendar of the year, and as a Wiccan, you will find harmony and abundance with each passing season due to that very truth: life begets death, which begets more life.

Moon cycles occur throughout each season and are celebrated throughout the Esbats ritual. The moon's cycles organise the seasons, and each waning moon ushers in an end, a darkening, while each waxing moon ushers in a powerful fullness with its own magic and ritual.

All of the rhythms and cycles are inherent in Wiccan work and will remain so in perpetuity. The concept of worshipping the divine in nature goes closely with the wheel of the year and should be counted as a major component of Wiccan worship.

Personal Responsibility and Responsibility

This concept is consistent with the Wiccan Rede and the Triple Law.

You are accountable for all of your actions. Wicca encourages you to be aware of your power, as it may be greater than you realise, especially when working with the sacred divine energies that pervade all things and all life.

When you practise Wicca, you take responsibility for more than just yourself; you harness the energy of all life to celebrate and support the life you live, and everything you do has an effect on others. It's also an excellent way for you to be candid about the truth of karma, because whatever you're accountable for in this life follows you into the next.

You are incredibly powerful, and Wicca assists you in embracing your internal strength and life force energy; it also requires you to be responsible with your strength, causing no harm and carrying out your rituals properly.

The Wiccan Rede: No Harm

The Wiccan Rede states simply that you should conduct your practise in such a way that it does not cause harm to another individual. While the golden rule of thumb is based on the principle of doing unto others, it also requires you to exercise extreme caution in your practise and to consider how you word your spells and rituals.

Wicca's practise is intended to benefit the greater good of all life, and thus a great deal of it is concerned with intentions. While practising, you may find that you need to state that you wish to cause no harm and that you will do everything possible to promote the well-being of all living things on Earth.

This credo is found in all Wiccan books and has remained consistent and true for a long period of time. It reminds you of your personal responsibility and power, as well as the fact that you must make the correct choice when utilising the gift of magic.

Equality

The Wiccan faith is not based on coercion. Propaganda is discouraged, and an aura of acceptance for all spiritual paths and backgrounds is embraced. Wiccans believe that equality is necessary in all aspects of life and that everyone has the right to follow their own spiritual path; the one that is right for them.

Although the concept of equality should be self-evident in all religions, this is frequently not the case. This is one of the ways in which Wicca is unique; it offers a path to receive wisdom and abundance through divine worship without implying that it must be done a certain way.

Wicca is synonymous with equality, and practising this artistic religion requires an open heart and mind toward anyone in need of a spiritual community and path.

Three-fold Rule

Numerous Wiccan traditions employ the Threefold Law, also known as the Rule of Three. While not everyone supports this law, it frequently comes up and should be noted, or practised, as the case may be. This concept states that whatever spell or magical act is performed, the energy generated by the act will enter the Universe and return three times to the practitioner.

You may or may not be familiar with this concept, which derives from other cultural practises, particularly those associated with Eastern religions that adhere to the law of karma. Wicca is what gives it the concept of three times, a number associated with the reality of the power wielded.

It may not occur in the manner in which you anticipate, for example, if you wish someone else harm, you may experience three separate instances of bad luck as a result, or it may feel as if the return is three times greater than it normally would be, such as expecting to receive $100 and receiving $300.

The Threefold Law is another tool to assist you in maintaining balance in your practise and ensuring that you do no harm, including harming yourself with the energy of three returning to you.

All Things Contain Elements

There are five elements in Wiccan belief: earth, air, fire, water, and ether, or spirit. During rituals and ceremonies, and particularly during the casting or consecrating of a circle, the five elements are invoked to bring the ritual's or spell's energies into balance. Not all Wiccans practise with all five elements and instead focus on the four primary ones, preserving spirit as represented by their deity.

These are the fundamental constituents of everything on Earth and in the Universe. They are accountable for the great eternal cycle of life, the birth-death-rebirth cycle. These sacred natural forces are an integral part of Wiccan practise because they are the literal life force that connects all matter and spirit.

These elements have been studied throughout history and were incorporated into philosophies dating all the way back to the early Greeks, who were also deity worshippers and followers of natural religions. These concepts are prevalent across continents and in a variety of religions and beliefs, including those of Egypt and Babylonia, Hinduism and Buddhism, and others.

The elements are unquestionably a tool that must be used in Wiccan practise, and as you gain a better understanding of your spell work and rituals, you will discover just how vital and powerful they can be.

Chapter 2
Wicca's Benefits

Wicca as a spiritual practise encompasses a wide variety of facets. There is no way to practise magic, and there will never be a way. People of all sects, cultures, and backgrounds practise magic for a variety of reasons.

Having said that, there are a number of basic characteristics that can benefit those who work. The following are twelve benefits of wick:

Almost Anyone Can Become A Wiccan – Although Wicca is frequently associated with the Wicca religion, one does not have to be a Wiccan to practise it.

Individuals of all religious backgrounds, as well as non-religious individuals, engage in sorcery.

There Are No Rules – Yes, there are spell books, manuals, resources, and a variety of things that people recommend, but the ritual is yours, and it can be as complicated or as simple as you like.

You Can Do It From Anywhere – A lot of Wiccans have named holy places and altars to practise spells, but in fact, they can be practiced anywhere. All you need is yourself, your objective, and a quiet space in which to concentrate.

Nature Time – One of Wicca's most significant benefits is that it encourages you to spend more time outdoors, interacting with nature, meditating, and developing a greater appreciation for your environment. Additionally, this provides an opportunity to unplug the phone.

Wicca requires extensive training, and you never truly stop learning. You'll learn a great deal about plants and their medicinal properties, the moon phases, nature, flowers, trees, and animals, crystals, yoga, chakras, natural healing, tea, mythology, and history, as well as the enchantment surrounding all of these things. You, too, should gain a better understanding of yourself!

Knowing What You Want – Spellwork requires you to be explicit about your objective, which can provide valuable insight into your life goals. As a result, it can assist you in taking additional action to address these issues.

Time To De-Stress – At its heart, Wicca is a spiritual practise centred on nature. Few things can ease our minds as Earth's children more than connecting with nature and the elements. Additionally, it enables regular meditation and thought.

There Are Numerous Paths – Because magic cannot be practised in isolation, you should choose the path that the majority of people identify with. You might be a hedge wick, a green wick, or a sea wick. You should gather in a coven or independently. You can either follow the spell books or create your own rituals.

There are numerous holy days that some Wiccans observe, including the summer and winter solstices, the spring and autumn equinoxes, Samhain, and Beltane. People celebrate in a variety of ways, but they frequently include cooking a special meal, attending ceremonies, taking nature walks, reflecting, remembering ancestors, lighting bonfires, and expressing gratitude.

Inspiration – Many wicks share their inspiration, positivity, and joy with others, and social media platforms make it simple to consume this wisdom.

It Is Inclusive – I believe that one of the reasons Wiccan resonates with so many people is that it is inclusive. This empowers women and is non-discriminatory toward LGBT individuals. This provides individuals with an opportunity to explore their faith in a judgement-free environment that also promotes compassion, self-care, harmony, and healing.

It Encourages the Development of Healthy Habits – Consuming tea, cooking with herbs, spending time outside, reading and dreaming, meditation, being honest about your desires, communicating with the environment, caring for the earth, caring for animals, reading books, and sharing your feelings are all things you can do more of as a Wiccan.

Chapter 3
Step by Step Guide to Rituals

Magik practise is simple. All you need are a few simple tools, an altar space, and clear intentions. The following step-by-step guide will assist you in becoming acquainted with the most fundamental forms of rituals, spells, and meditations. You are not required to follow these rules in order to cast; you may use them as a starting point and source of inspiration for creating your own potent rituals and spells.

Wicca is heavily reliant on intuition and connection to one's higher self, as well as one's own divine wisdom and authority. Allow yourself to be your guide as you determine the most effective methods for invoking the appropriate power, energy, and intention in order to attract more abundance and prosperity into your life.

As you begin, search your home for some of these tools.

You are not required to rush out to the store and purchase a slew of new items in order to construct your altar or prepare your spells. Much of what you'll need can be found around the house until something better, or more purposeful, becomes available.

Your Toolbox

A witch's basic tool kit is composed of only a few items, which are listed below. There are additional items that you can consider optional until you have accumulated your tool chest of magical properties and elements.

- Candle(s)/holder for a candle
- Lighters/matches
- Salt
- Minerals/crystals (optional)
- Smudge stick or incense (preferably sage)
- A glass or wooden bowl of purified water (not plastic)

These are the only tools you truly require to get started. As you gain experience and proficiency, you can incorporate symbolic elements into your ritual or spell casting. Certain Wiccans prefer to keep figurines of their preferred deities for personal use or to place on the altar they create. Additionally, you may incorporate additional herbs into the ritual as desired, but ultimately, all that is required are the items on the list above.

These tools do not require an altar to be used. You can even take them out into nature or wherever you are casting magik and use them as a travelling toolbox for creating magik.

The candle adds fire to your ceremony, which is one of the elements you'll need to summon into your circle. The matches and lighter will be used to light the candle(s) and incense. Salt is an extremely effective protective agent. Some people cast their circles by encircling their bodies and tools with salt, but you can also keep it with you in a box or tin as a representation of the Earth's energy and as a protective symbol.

Although the stones and crystals are optional, they can be useful for magnifying and intensifying energy; thus, whatever ritual or spell you are performing, your chosen stones/crystals can help enhance the experience and add more energy to it. Each stone and crystal has its own distinct properties, and determining which ones resonate the most with you will be an integral part of your journey.

The incense/smudge stick is used to purify the energy in the room and to cleanse your own auras. It can be used prior to, during, and after your ritual to assist you in feeling balanced and attuned to your spells.

Candles

Candles are an integral part of any ritual. Since we learned how to create our own lasting light, we have all used candles, and the candle is a powerful symbol of life in the practise of Wicca.

The act of lighting a candle creates a strong energetic vibration of intention, allowing you to connect more deeply with the powerful magick you wish to invoke. Including candles in all of your ritual and spell work helps to direct that energy and focus.

Occasionally, you may wish to keep a candle in a container to burn overnight or until it burns out. Allowing the sacred flame of your spell work to burn continuously demonstrates energetically that your intentions will endure until the next candle is lit.

Additionally, you'll want to find candles whose colours correspond to those in your spells. The following is a list of possible meanings for each candle colour in a spell you are working:

White – Purity, harmony, peace, cleansing, innocence, balance, healing, magic involving small children, spirituality, and aura balancing

Yellow – Success, joy, pleasure, concentration, learning, solar/sun magick, confidence, travel, memory, imagination, and flexibility, element of air

Orange – Possibilities, creativity, joy, investments, legal

matters, justice, self-expression, addiction recovery, business success, ambition, vitality, and enjoyment

Pink – Symbolizes feminine energy, compassion, love, romance, domestic bliss, partnerships, friendships, child protection, nurturing, and self-improvement.

Red – Vitality, passion, courage, sexual potency, fertility, and survival, as well as the fire element, independence, conflict, competition, and war.

Purple – Contact with spirits, independence, wisdom, influence, breaking bad habits, altering fortunes, banishing evil energy or dark forces, spiritual strength

Blue – Concentration, forgiveness, communication, truth, fidelity, fortune, astral projection, water element, sincerity, patience, domestic harmony, and raising negative/low vibrations.

Green – Physical and emotional healing, good fortune, growth, acceptance, marriage, prosperity, abundance, dispel/counteract envy or greed, tree and plant magick.

Brown – Earth magick and the earth element, stability, material possessions or wealth, construction, real estate/house magik, house blessings, animal and pet magik

Black – Protection, security, warding off black magic, reversing hexes, defence, banishing negative vibrations, grounding, wisdom, scrying, and pride

Silver – Psychic perception, lucid dreams and dream states, meditation, communication, feminine energies, victory, stability, moon magic, and gambling luck

Gold – Masculine energies, abundance, prosperity, sun/solar energy, positive vibrations, divination, great fortune, attraction, luxury, health, and justice

You are not required to use vibrant candles to cast spells or perform rituals. Any type of candle will work, and you may use them in any manner that feels safe and appropriate. Using coloured candles will give your spell and craft work an extra boost of energy and intention. Color and candle magick are both extremely potent and powerful energies that, when combined, create a great force of light and alignment with your practice's intentions.

Smudging

Smudging is an ancient ceremonial practise in which sacred herbs are burned to produce a pungent and aromatic smoke that cleanses and purifies. Utilizing a smudge stick or bundle of dried herbs in your ceremonies is extremely beneficial and should be done as frequently as possible.

When you incorporate a smudge stick into your spells and rituals, you are energetically cleansing the space around you and shielding your energy from any unwanted energies that may be drawn to you. You can draw a large circle around the area where you will be casting with the smoke from your smudge stick. You can also use salt in this manner, but the mess is frequently more difficult to clean up, unless you are outside.

Smudging is a lovely ceremonial tool that can be used prior to, during, or after incantations and rituals. The following are some of the most popular smudge sticks: Sage Cedar

Sweet fescue
Lavender

Palo Santo Juniper Mugwort (sacred wood, not herbs)
Any of these would be appropriate for your ceremonies and crafts. Even better, you can create your own. All you need is your preferred herb. While it is still fresh, tie it in a bundle with string.

Dry it upside down. Utilize as needed.

Crystals and Stones

Each stone and crystal has its own unique properties and characteristics.

Some are beneficial for protection and grounding, while others are beneficial for enhancing spiritual connection and opening the third eye.

It is highly recommended to work with a variety of stones and crystals because they all have very different vibrations and meanings. There are hundreds of thousands of different types of stones, and you may have to enjoy a little digging and research to find the one that is the best fit for your specific needs.

Conduct an experiment to determine the appropriate stones and crystals: Locate a local shop that specialises in the sale of stones and crystals in your area.

While in the shop, use your dominant magical hand (which may or may not be your dominant writing hand) to hover over the stones to which you are drawn. Allow your intuition to guide you. If you are drawn to a particular stone, pick it up and observe how it feels. If you feel a strong energy in the palm of your hand, the stone or crystal is resonating with your vibration and will be beneficial to work with.

Everything in your toolkit is designed to assist you in developing a stronger connection to the greater energies and spirits of the world around you. Consider how these tools make you feel energetically attuned to the task at hand as you work with them. At times, you may resonate more with the fire element and desire more candlelight in your practise; at other times, you may feel drawn to incorporate more Earthly items from nature into your castings or to conduct your rituals in the woods.

All of the elements play a significant role in your Wicca practise, which is why developing relationships with these tools is critical. The work you do with nature's energy brings you closer to yourself and to all of the energies that are here to assist and guide you on your path. Develop a toolkit that feels authentic to you and take pleasure in practising your rituals with your sacred and magical elements.

Establishing Your Altar

An altar is a place of worship dedicated to something. It can be anything you wish, and constructing your altar is an artistic expression of your magik and practise. Each of us requires a space in our homes that reflects our deepest desires and passions, as well as our thoughts and expectations. An altar is an excellent way to manifest your spiritual journey physically.

There are no rules for arranging your altar, and it will frequently change as you grow and evolve. It adopts the life you are living as you add and subtract items from it in accordance with your intentions and practises.

Altars are a reflection of who you are and what you pray to, so as you create your own, be mindful of how it reflects the values you have chosen to align with at all times. It must have a sense of flow and an energy of harmony and balance. You may need to tend to your altar daily or on a more frequent basis in order to maintain its energy and ability to attract abundance into your life.

Your altar should be located in an area of your home that is inaccessible to others but visible to you, so that you are always aware of it. Many people place altars in plain view, which is perfectly acceptable; they do not need to be hidden; they simply require space to exist undisturbed by anyone except you.

Your altar can be placed on a bookshelf, in a cabinet, on top of your dresser, or even hung on the wall. It is entirely up to you to determine the proper location for your altar. Once you've identified the ideal location, you can begin gathering the materials necessary to construct and decorate it.

Often, people will spread a cloth out on the surface of the area where the cloth will sit. It could be something small, such as a scarf or handkerchief, or something more meaningful, such as a piece of Grandmother's heirloom lace. You are not required to use a cloth, but if you do, make sure it reflects the overall energy of your altar.

Following that, you can begin bringing in objects that will assist you in remaining aligned with your spiritual path and purpose. Many people display sculptures or figurines of their favourite gods and goddesses, while others display paintings, photographs, or other works of art in tribute to a particular deity. Anything goes, and it all depends on your preferences and desired focus.

Another option is to simply use the tools in your tool kit. You can arrange these items on the altar and dedicate this space to sacred rituals, ensuring that your tools are always on display. Essentially, you're constructing an altar for your magical implements. By highlighting these items on an altar, you will be reminded of the importance of working with this magik and will be able to continue honouring your Wiccan practise. When you're ready to work with your tools, you can begin by lighting candles on your altar, burning incense, or smudging the altar, and then begin your rituals.

Your altar is essentially a manifestation of your inner magical self. It reflects your strength and curiosity to inquire about the great unknown and to worship the energy that pervades all things in this world.

Bring to your altar anything that is currently resonating with you.

You could choose to decorate it with fresh cut flowers and allow them to wilt and dry to symbolise life and death.

Additionally, you may wish to gather items during your nature walks to dedicate the altar to Mother Earth. It can also be a place that changes with each Wiccan holiday celebration, transforming your altar into a shrine to the Earth's seasons and rhythms.

Make no apprehensions about altering your altar. It may change along with you as you mature, and it will require the same level of care as you do for yourself.

Treat it as if it were alive and as an extension of yourself. Whatever water you choose to keep on your altar, if any, it must be clean and pure; allowing it to become dirty and stagnant is a sign that you are neglecting your altar and spiritual practise.

Attend to it and allow it to be a constant source of transformation in your life, eliciting a more spiritual reflection of your journey.

Invoking the Assistance of the Gods/Goddesses

Whether you seek guidance from the gods and goddesses of Pagan ritual or not, allowing yourself to be open to their assistance and guidance is an excellent way to connect with the energies of all things as you practise Wicca. You may not work with a specific deity or dedicate your altar to one, but as you prepare your rituals, it is a good idea to signal to the universal energies that you are willing to tap in and accept assistance if it is offered as you cast your spells and perform your rituals.

Simply say the following words as you light the candles and burn the incense on your altar: "I am opening the lights of all life to the energy of all things." I pray to the Great Mother and Father for guidance, support, and protection, as well as for all offerings from the spirits and deities of all life. As I progress through my ritual, I am open to receiving your love, light, and warmth. Thus shall it be."

You can change the wording to whatever feels right for you, depending on the energies you wish to call in for assistance. You may be more drawn to fairy magic or to working with spirit guides from the animal kingdom. Additionally, you may wish to establish a connection with your forefathers and mothers as you begin your rituals and spell castings. All of these ways of connecting to that work will benefit you, so choose one that is compatible with your unique Wiccan practise.

Change the wording of the preceding message to reflect your practise while maintaining the message's integrity. Declaring your willingness to receive assistance and guidance is a very effective connection tool.

Maintaining a desire to work exclusively with light and love energies is critical because it indicates that you wish to work with higher vibrations and do not wish to invoke anything harmful or low energy, such as a trickster spirit or energy that may not be as helpful as other energies.

Allowing yourself to be open to all of this will assist you in concentrating even more on your intentions and the goals of your spells. Relax, ask for assistance, and express gratitude to all the energies that come to assist you along your path.

Circulation of Your Circle

You are not required to cast your circle using your altarpiece. You may be out in the woods at the time of casting and will be a long way from your altar. It is possible that you will only use your altar to store your magical tools between castings and will not need to incorporate it into your Wicca work; however, you may feel more grounded in your practises if you begin by connecting with the energy of your altar prior to casting your circle. How you choose to work with your own energy and magical tools is entirely up to you.

What is the purpose of casting a circle, and what does it even mean? When you invoke the energies around you and connect your own energy to the spiritual plane, you must have an intention and protection opening and closing. It not only assists you in maintaining clarity and focus while performing rituals and casting spells, but it also acts as a deliberate centering of your energy and attachment to your spiritual self. Casting is similar to meditating in order to re-engage you with your work.

Casting a circle in your preparation also serves as a way to align yourself with the four directions and the four elements. Each path you take is represented by a circle, and each element of your life spark is represented to help you connect to your full potential and purpose. When you cast a circle, you are acknowledging your journey and bringing into focus what assists you on your path: the directions and the elements.

Keep in mind that while practising, you should create an

environment that feels healthy and balanced to you. It is preferable to do so in a location where you will not be interrupted or disturbed. The steps below will assist you in casting your circle of intention and protection.

1. If you are working in close proximity to your altar and wish to incorporate it into your ritual, you can begin by lighting candles on the altar and lighting your smudge stick to cleanse the altar's and your own energy.

2. Facing north, say the following words: "I invoke the north's energy." You are cordially invited to join this circle of light. Thus it is."

3. Facing east, say the following words: "I invoke the east's energy." You are cordially invited to join this circle of light. Thus it is."

4. Facing south, say the following words: "I invoke the south's energy." You are cordially invited to join this circle of light. Thus it is."

   Address the west with the following words: "I invoke the west's energy." You are cordially invited to join this circle of light. Thus it is."

   **NOTE: You may alter the wording of these phrases to suit your purposes. They are a condensed version of what you can say to announce the entrance of the four directions into your circle, and as you progress and become more creative with your practise, you may wish to add some additional information to how you call upon the directions.

5. Now that you've summoned the directions, you can invite the elements to your current location. You may choose to keep your elements on the altar or spread them out on the

table you are seated at or on the ground if you are seated at that level. This section may require the use of specific tools and objects, and if possible, lay the corresponding element in the directional position with which it is aligned. For instance, if your element is earth, position your dish of salt or soil to the north.

6. Place your earth element in the north position (or wherever you are sitting) and say the following: "I invoke the earth's energy as I cast my circle of protection and power."
    You are cordially invited to join this circle of light. Thus it is."

7. Proceed with Step 7 in the same manner as you did with Steps 2-5, arranging an object or representation for each element. East represents air; south represents fire; and west represents water. For air, you can either use a smoking incense or smudge stick or place bird feathers in this position. A candle works well for the south and fire positions, while a dish of clean, clear water works well for the west.

8. As a substitute for these items, crystals or stones that resonate with the directional energies could be used; one stone or crystal for each direction representing the elements.

    The final step in casting the circle can be a personal declaration, such as the following: "I awaken to the energies of the four directions and four elements and cast this circle of protection and light with their assistance and guidance as I work with their energies." Thus shall it be."

**NOTE: The phrases 'So mote it be' and 'and thus it is' are synonymous. It is the force of asserting, 'and this is true.' By including it at the end of an intentional phrase, you can create a very strong energetic assignment for whatever magic you are performing. Both are equally effective and can be used interchangeably.

You have now taken the first step toward delving deeper into the ritual and spell casting that you have chosen. Develop a sense of comfort with your preferred method of casting your circle and repeat it consistently.

Casting a circle of protection and power is a ritual unto itself, and your own personal circle casting should be unique to you. Utilize the steps above to create your own version of casting a circle and have fun with it!

Intentions, Spells, and Rituals

The next step in the typical spell or ritual process is the actual spell or ritual work that brings you into alignment with your intentions.

Bear in mind that it is critical to enter with clear intentions, so before you cast your circle, ask yourself: What is my magical purpose for today?

Once you've established what you want to accomplish or focus on, you can either design your ritual or spell from scratch or use pre-existing spells and craft work that feel natural and appropriate for the task at hand. There are countless spells available online and in books that can assist you in determining the best way for you to align with your craft work.

Much of what you will do in this step will be defining and stating your intentions for generating the energy of life. It may contain herbs and other substances that bolster your intention. If you're honouring a holiday or a particular god or goddess, you'll be utilising specific items and energies to bolster your ritual or spell.

Words are significant, and you may wish to write down the words you wish to share once the circle has been opened.

Preparation is just as critical as execution of your ritual or spell.

Prior to opening your circle, jot down your spell's words on a scrap of paper. Collect the herbs you wish to include in your circle, as well as any relics or objects that hold significance for you.

There are countless unique ways to invoke your own potent magik and make it known to the energies that surround you. The following steps are intended to provide you with simple ideas and pointers on how to begin creating your ritual and spell.

Bear in mind that practising Wicca is a creative and artistic endeavour, and there is no one correct way to do it. The following steps will assist you in getting started with creating a spell and/or ritual.

1. Establish your intent. It can be written on paper, leaves, stones or pieces of wood for burning, or on anything magical.

2. Collect all of your ingredients. You may be utilising herbal remedies to assist you in accomplishing your goal. Make a bouquet of them and place them on your altar to dry. Collect appropriate stones, crystals, and other earth elements and place them where they feel most at ease.

3. After casting your circle of protection and power, you may wish to collect sacred water from a waterfall or a river that feels magical to you. Utilizing your written intentions as a declaration is an excellent way to open yourself up to the energy of the task at hand. Do not simply write it on the paper or on the leaves; read it aloud so that you can feel the words coming out of your mouth with sound and releasing them into your circle.

4. Set intentions and make declarations using your candles, incense, crystals, or other ritual objects. For instance, if you

are working with fire magic, you may have chosen a specific number of coloured candles to represent the energy you wish to invoke. While lighting each candle, you can say, "As I light this candle, I invite the power of fire to bless my ritual and invoke the passion of firelight to assist me on my path."

**NOTE: Because everything you do carries energy and intention, even lighting a candle requires you to make declarations about what you are doing aloud to ensure that the energy in your ritual is clear.

5. Apply the same concept from Step 4 to the remaining elements of your ritual or spell casting. For instance, if you have sacred river water to incorporate into your ritual, you can say something along the lines of: "As this water flows into this cup, allow it to flow through me with intention and energy to fulfil my purpose."
   Indeed, it is!"
6. Once you've incorporated all of your spell's ingredients, you can recite, or speak aloud, your spell's words of intention and incantation.

Assume you're casting a prosperity spell. Simply state, "Here on this day, I invoke the life force energy of prosperity." The candle will burn continuously throughout the night and day, aligning me with the fortune I seek. Water will flow from this chalice until I am blessed. Every day and night, I will burn smoke to welcome the gift of abundance. I'm going to shake salt onto these coins in order to gain more of what I'm after. Prosperity! Indeed, it is!"

Any spells or rituals you perform will be enjoyable, unique, and tailored to the purpose of the work you are doing. Once you have a basic understanding of how to open a circle and manifest your magical intentions, you will have the freedom to explore additional possibilities for finding and creating your own spells and rituals.

Even if you discover popular spells online or in other books, you can always add to or modify them to meet your specific needs. No harm will come to you if you alter existing spells.

Wicca is a creative practise that requires only your commitment to the light of your truth and your inner knowing as you walk the Wiccan path.

Circulating Within Your Circle

It's just as simple to close your circle as it is to open it. All that is required is that you show respect and gratitude to the elements and directions. You may wish to face each direction once more and ask for their assistance in guiding you along your path while your spell takes effect.

Additionally, you can connect with the elements in your space and carefully return them to their altar space to bring closure to them. Here are a few steps to assist you in closing your circle once it has been opened:

1. Express gratitude to each element directly. Ex: I'm grateful to the earth for grounding me (sprinkle salt or soil into your hands and rub them together, allowing the salt/soil to naturally fall away).

   I'd like to express my gratitude to the air that propels me forward on my journey (put out the smudge stick). Many thanks to the fire that illuminates my path (blow out candle). We give thanks for the cleansing and purifying power of water (dip fingers in water and flick on your altar or on your own face).

2. As with the elements in Step 1, stand up or direct your energy in the direction of each of the four directions to express gratitude for their presence. All you have to do is express gratitude and proceed through each direction, completing the circle in the same manner as it began.

3. Alternatively, you can combine Steps 1 and 2 and complete the circle by simultaneously thanking each direction and corresponding element.

4. A final expression of gratitude can be made to the Great Mother and Father, or to whichever gods/goddesses you invoked in your ritual.

5. The concluding words: "And thus it is!" or "And thus shall it be!"

Acceptance of Your True Strength

Wicca is a lovely, enjoyable, and magical way to connect with your true power and the energy that pervades all life. It has a way of inviting you to be present and to identify your entire being and the nature of the thing you seek with a mindful appreciation for nature and all of her energies.

One of the most profound lessons of Wicca and other Pagan practises is that they enable you to explore yourself and your inner power creatively as you transform and grow. The most effective way for you to approach rituals and spell casting is to trust your inner guidance regarding how the spell should proceed and the possible outcomes.

There are numerous variations on a single intention or spell, because there is no incorrect way to cast. As long as you adhere to the Wiccan Rede, virtually anything is permissible. As you continue to work on your own spells and rituals, remember to prioritise your power. Devotions to the Earth Mother and all other gods and goddesses are just as vital as devotion to your own magical abilities and truths.

Have fun creating your own spells and grimoires! A grimoire is simply a collection of magical spells and invocations that you can create at any time. Each spell you perform can be meticulously documented in your own book of magic that is unique to you and the traditions or beliefs you choose to follow.

Working on your own grimoire is a unique way to devote yourself to your magical path, and having a reference to your own book of spell work can be beneficial in the future when you want to repeat or enhance spells that you have already created and performed.

It is very traditional for a witch to create his or her own grimoire, and so while you are immersing yourself in your Wiccan experience, pick up a notebook and begin a journal of your recipes and incantations for future reference and use. It's a beneficial way to develop confidence in your own magic and true power.

Chapter 4
Love and Relationship Spells

Affirmation for New Friendships

Whether you've recently moved to a new area and don't know many people, or your social life is in desperate need of an overhaul, this quick spell introduces you to new people with whom you can form friendships if you so desire.

It's best to perform this ritual during a waxing moon, but if you have an upcoming social encounter that you'd like to infuse with magical energy, by all means, do not wait until the moon is waning.

You will require the following:

- 1 petite piece of rose quartz, clear quartz, carnelian, or lapis lazuli

- 1 yellow votive or spell candle
- Essential oil of lavender

Instructions:
- Use the oil to anoint the candle.
- Place the stone in the palm of your dominant hand and place your other hand on top.
- Close your eyes and visualise yourself surrounded by positive people who are enjoyable and reassuring to be around.
- Once you've captured this sensation, inhale deeply, exhale fully, and open your eyes.
- Place the stone in front of the candle and then light the wick while saying these words: "New and true friendships, may our kindred souls unite."
- Carry the stone with you whenever you leave the house and leave it in a prominent location for when you return.

Attractiveness for Attracting High-Quality Relationships

Coriander has a warm, fragrant, slightly nutty flavour when used in cooking. However, not everyone is aware that coriander is actually the seed of the cilantro herb.

Interestingly, the seed and the leaf have completely different flavours. Coriander's dual nature is reflected in its magical properties, which include attracting love and protecting against negative energies.

The seed is used in love spells, aphrodisiac potions, and for reconciling feuding parties, as well as for exorcism and home protection. And, because it's readily available in the spice aisle of most supermarkets, it's an excellent herb for beginning kitchen Witches to work with.

This spell utilises both the attractive and protective properties of coriander to help you attract new potential partners into your life in a balanced manner.

This is especially beneficial for those who appear to have no difficulty attracting admirers but have significant difficulty maintaining relationships. Coriander's energy ensures that those who are ultimately harmful to you do not enter your sphere of awareness, while those who present a positive, healthy, compatible match have an easy path to you.

By including rose quartz in the mix, the spell's positive vibration is amplified. Purchase whole coriander seeds rather than coriander powder, as you will be carrying the herb.

You will require the following:

- 13 coriander seeds, whole
- 1 miniature rose quartz
- 1 small drawstring bag or fabric scrap
- 1 ribbon, either red or pink
- 1 work candle (optional—for atmosphere)

Instructions:

- If using a candle, light it.
- Coriander seeds should be arranged in a circle around the rose quartz.
- Close your eyes and picture yourself completely at ease with a partner who accepts you for who you are.
- When you've established a connection with this sensation, open your eyes, focus on the rose quartz, and repeat the following (or similar) phrase: "I draw to be nothing less than healthy, balanced love."
- Collect the coriander seeds one at a time, placing them in the drawstring bag or cloth. (It is best to begin with the seed in the circle's southernmost point and work your way clockwise.)
- Add the rose quartz and secure the bag or cloth with the ribbon.
- Bring the charm along whenever you're in the mood to take a chance on love—especially when you're out in public.

Attraction to Romance Smudge

This is a fun, easy ritual for enhancing the atmosphere in your home or any other space where romance is desired!

You will require the following:
- 1 crimson candle
- A dried lavender sprig or a smudge stick made entirely of lavender
- Rose absolute essential oil (optional)
- a single feather (optional)

Instructions:
- If using rose oil, anoint the candle with a drop or two. Wipe your fingers clean of any excess oil, and then light the candle.
- As you say the following (or similar) words, ignite the lavender sprig or smudge stick from the candle flame: "Loving lavender, creative fire, charge this space with love's desire."
- Beginning in the northern part of the room, move in a clockwise circle, fanning the lavender smoke with the feather (if using) or your hand to ensure that it spreads as widely as possible throughout the room. If you wish, you may repeat the above-mentioned powerful words aloud as a chant as you walk.
- Allow the lavender to burn out naturally in a fire-resistant dish if possible; if not, gently extinguish it with a potted plant or bowl of sand.

Exceptional First Date Charming Confidence

This spell is for you if you're the type who gets nervous before meeting a potential love interest for the first time.

Simply carry the charm in your pocket or purse—you may want to enclose it in a drawstring bag or piece of cloth if you're carrying it with other items to keep it secure.

Bear in mind that the emphasis is on your own confidence and sense of self-worth, regardless of how the other person is. If you have a good time regardless of the outcome, the spell was successful.

You will require the following:
- One pink or white ribbon, approximately seven inches in length
- One small carnelian or tiger's eye
- Sodium chloride
- One candle for work (optional)
- A small drawstring bag or swatch of cloth (optional)

Instructions:
- If using a candle, light it.
- Arrange the ribbon in a pleasing pattern on your altar or workspace.
- Construct a circle of sea salt around the ribbon—this will focus the spell's energy on the charm.
- Place the stone on the ribbon and say the following (or something similar): "My confidence radiates from within; I am at ease in my own skin." This coming together of souls will be a joy. I charm this stone for added protection."
- Gently wrap the ribbon around the stone and secure with a knot.
- Now go out and have some fun meeting new people!

Bath Ritual for a Blind Date

Whether you're on a blind date set up by a friend or venturing into the world of online dating, meeting someone new can be nerve-wracking.

This spell virtually guarantees that you will have a good time, by sublimating nervousness and promoting self-confidence, which will enhance the encounter's energy regardless of the outcome.

Indeed, you will have a good time even if it becomes clear at the conclusion that there will be no second date!

While Himalayan salt is an excellent relaxant, it can be quite potent and induce sleepiness if not used regularly. Therefore, if you're taking this bath in the days leading up to the date, you may want to opt for the sea salt.

If your tub has a mesh catch-all drain, the herbs can be sprinkled liberally. Alternatively, contain them in a teabag or a thin washcloth to prevent them from spreading into the water.

You will require the following:
- 1 teaspoon to 1 tablespoon hibiscus
- 1 teaspoon to 1 tablespoon chamomile
- Coltsfoot or red clover, 1 tsp. to 1 tbsp.
- 2 to 3 tbsp. Sea salt or Himalayan salt
- 5 mL lavender essential oil
- Approximately one citrine, aventurine, or tiger's eye
- A candle(s) for ambience

Instructions:
- Run the bath until it is about a quarter full, then add the salt.
- Fill the tub halfway with water and add the crystal of your choice.
- Add the herbs to the bath when it is nearly full.
- Light the candle(s), turn off the bathroom's artificial lighting, and climb in.
- Remain relaxed and consciously let go of any anxiety you may be experiencing as a result of meeting this new

person. Additionally, let go of any attachments you may have to the desired outcome.

- Maintain a minimum of 20 minutes in the bath. If possible, remain in the tub while draining the water, as this allows the energy of the herbs and crystal to work more effectively.
- Bring the crystal on your date, and have fun!

Divine "Forecast" of Relationship Potential

For singles, meeting a new potential love interest can be both exciting and perplexing.

Even if you appear to "click" with this person, you are still operating in an environment where far more unknown information exists than known information. It's difficult to avoid wondering whether things will work out as planned, and it's easy to get caught up in over-analyzing even the smallest details.

Perhaps you're concerned that the person is "too good to be true," or that you'll rush into something. Alternatively, you may be attempting to talk yourself out of a potentially wonderful relationship solely because it will require you to step outside your comfort zone. Perhaps it's a combination of all of the above?

The issue, of course, is that overthinking it actually impairs your ability to see clearly and can result in increased confusion, rather than less. This spell can assist you in determining whether your new prospect has sufficient romantic potential to warrant further mental energy investment.

You may receive a straightforward yes or no, but you may also receive additional information that assists you in making your own decision or a signal that you should remain open and detached from any particular outcome for the time being. Whatever your "forecast" proves to be, this spell will move the energy from a state of immobility to one of resolution by assisting you in getting out of your own way!

Any of the three crystals listed below is suitable for this spell, but if you have all three and are unsure which to use, here are some finer energetic points to consider for your specific situation:

• Malachite is especially helpful if your current confusion or concern is rooted in a previous relationship experience.
• Quartz is an excellent all-purpose intuition booster and aids in clearing inner turmoil;
• Amethyst aids in dispelling illusions and controlling "obsessive thinking."

You will require the following:
- One amethyst, quartz crystal, or malachite of small to medium size
- A solitary scrap of paper
- One candle with a fragrance (optional)

Instructions:
- If using a candle, light it.
- Spend some time grounding and centering yourself. For the time being, set aside any actual thoughts about the person.
- On the strip of paper, write the person's name and request that any and all illusions you may have about the person be removed.
- (Avoid asking specific questions; otherwise, your mental energy will contaminate the spell.)
- You might want to say the following (or something similar): "Infinite intelligence of the Universe, please illuminate the path that I am meant to see in relation to [name of person] and me."
- Fold the paper several times until it fits comfortably beneath the crystal, and place it on your altar with the crystal atop.
- When you retire for the night, place the crystal (along with the paper) beneath your pillow. You will almost certainly

receive additional information in your dreams, but don't worry if this does not occur—you will receive information of some sort in your waking life within the next 48 hours.

Choosing Peace in Adversity

At some point in our lives, we all face enormous obstacles over which we have no control. It could be that a family member is battling a serious illness, or that a major world event has wreaked havoc on your life.

While it is always acceptable to work magic to exert whatever influence you can on the outcome of a situation, doing so from a place of empowerment can be difficult when you are personally affected, negating the spell's energy.

In times like these, you must first look after yourself before you can help others.

This spell is best performed for about an hour before bedtime. If you prefer to let your spell candles burn down completely on their own, you must place them in a sink before going to bed!

Alternatively, you may gently extinguish the candle and repeat the spell on subsequent nights until the candle is completely consumed.

This spell is truly meant to be customised to your liking.

Put on some meditative music, brew some chamomile tea, stretch your limbs, take a hot bath, and/or do whatever else helps you relax. The more "prepped" you are energetically for this spell, the more powerful it will be.

You will require the following:
- Consciousness 1 white candle 1 oil blend
- Music for contemplation (optional)

Instructions:
- Turn on the music, if using, and take any other measures necessary to bring yourself back to a state of calm.

- Take a few deep breaths and sit quietly. Use the oil to anoint your pulse points and the candle.

- Close your eyes and take a few more deep breaths, attempting to clear your mind completely.

- When you are ready, open your eyes and light the candle while saying the following (or similar): I release this burden to my higher power and redirect my focus on balance and rest. Therefore, allow it to be.

- For several moments, sit and gaze at the candle flame, keeping your mind as quiet as possible and your focus on the light.

Spell for Spiritual Connection Using a "Spare Key"

Although we typically think of "relationship" in terms of other people, we also have a relationship with our "higher power" — or whatever term you prefer for the force that moves through you when performing magic. This spell is intended to strengthen that relationship, which is ultimately the basis for all human relationships.

While it is becoming less common in today's world, many households have long kept a spare key outside the house, whether under the doormat, in a potted plant, or in some other concealed location. This serves as a backup in the event of a lost key and as a means of granting access to relatives or friends while the homeowner is away.

This spell invokes the wisdom and trust energies inherent in this tradition as a way of paying tribute to the benevolent forces working for you in the unseen realms.

By blessing and burying a key outside near your home (or indoors in a potted plant, if necessary), you are communicating to your higher power—whether a deity, a guardian spirit, or simply the benevolent energy of the Universe—that you welcome their presence and assistance in your home and life, regardless of where you are at any given moment.

Additionally, it serves as a reminder to yourself that even if you temporarily lose contact with your spiritual centre, you will always be able to reconnect.

Depending on the level of crime in your neighbourhood, you may feel more secure using a genuine spare key to your home, but any metal key will suffice for this spell.

Certain individuals prefer to use a gold key to symbolise God and/or a silver key to symbolise the Goddess (using two keys is perfectly fine).

You will require the following:
- a single key
- 1 white pillar candle

Instructions:
- While meditating quietly for several minutes, hold the key in your hands.
- Concentrate on the sensation of being truly connected to your authentic self and higher power.
- When you are ready, light the candle and say the following (or similar) words: "[Name of deity/spirit/higher power], you are welcome in my home and heart now and forever." From this day forward, let this key represent your and my access to my highest self."
- Three times quickly pass the key through the candle flame (avoid allowing the key to become hot to protect your fingers).
- Then bury it at least six inches underground outside your home or in the soil of a large potted plant.

Chapter 5
Herbal Magic: Rituals and Spells

You can incorporate tens of thousands of magical rituals and spells into your herbal magic practise. This chapter will highlight some of the ways in which you can use herbs for casting spells, brewing potions, and a variety of other purposes. In the final chapter, you'll learn about additional healing brews and potions, but keep in mind that they're just as magical as the recipes you're about to read. All of your herbal craft work contains magic, and these rituals and spells add an exciting new dimension to your Wicca Herbal Magic practise.

Tea Infusion with Magical Properties for Use in Any Potion or Brew

Many of these elixirs are actually just plain tea. The previous chapter included several examples of healing tea potions that can be used in times of sickness or health, and with this simple Tea Infusion Ritual, you can infuse even more magic into any of those brews. Utilize it daily for any type of tea you wish to brew. The magical energy you use to charge all of your spells and remedies will bring you inner fulfilment.

How to Prepare and Enjoy a Magical Tea (Infusion)

To empower your tea, follow these steps:

1. While steeping the potion, visualise yourself completely enveloped in light (choose the colour according to the magical effect you require). For example, green is associated with healing; pink with love; and orange with strength.)

2. Visualize the same coloured light emanating from the potion as you pour and drink it.

3. Visualize the light emanating from within you, flowing through your entire body, and then out into the world around you after you drink.

4. Visualize it reaching upward (as above) and downward (as below), extending your will and desire into the universe.

5. While drinking the tea and visualising the light, you can recite a mantra or affirmation for your Tea Spell.

Constructing a Mystical Tincture

You've already read Chapter 3's instructions for making a tincture, and this spell and ritual will assist you in infusing your tinctures with an energy charge and a magical intention or purpose. Each time you shake your jar of herbal alcohol potion (twice daily for a month), you will infuse it with the necessary magical energy via this tincture charging spell.

Charge Your Tinctures with a Spell and Ritual

You'll require the following:
- 1 green candle—represents the spirits of herbs
- 1 white candle - to honour the spirit and the power of magic
- 1 wick for charging the tincture- The colour selected is determined by the spell being worked mixing bowl – glass or stainless steel, no plastic
- Herbs and tincture alcohol (or alcohol substitute)
- 2 jars mason
- Cheesecloth

1. On your altar or wherever you are performing your ritual, form a triangle with your candles. Place the white candle at the triangle's top point, furthest away from you, and the green and other candles at the triangle's base points. The white candle point is used to direct energy away from you and into the Universe.

2. Center the bowl on your altar in the triangle of candles. Your herbs and alcohol (or substitute) should be nearby but not in the bowl yet.

3. As you light the white candle, make the following statement: "For the spirit's strength."

4. Declare the following as you light the white candle: "For the herbal spirits."

5. Using the final coloured candle and your requirements for this tincture spell, light the candle and state your intention as you did with the previous two candles.

6. For each herb that you intend to use in your tincture, you will premeasure your ingredients prior to beginning your

ritual. After lighting the candles, measure each herb one by one and place it in the bowl on the altar, offering a blessing of gratitude and stating your need for that particular herb.

7. Repeat this ritual for each herb you add to the bowl. Stir the mixture clockwise as you add each herb to ensure complete incorporation. In this practise, the clockwise direction is the direction for increasing or bringing something to you.
Counterclockwise would be the reduction or elimination of excess in your life.

8. Once all of the herbs have been added and stirred, place your hand over the bowl and state your magical intention and purpose.

9. Depending on your need and most likely the colour candle you've chosen for your specific spell, imagine and visualise that colour of light emanating from your hands and charging the herb mixture on the altar. (For example, love is represented by a pink light; money is represented by a green light, and so forth.)

10. Remove your herbs from the lit candles and place them in your mason jar along with the alcohol. Lids should be used to secure the jars.

11. Remove the mixing bowl from the altar and replace it with the jar of herb and alcohol mixture in the centre of the candle triangle. Maintain this position for the jar until all of the candles have burned out.

12. After the candles have been extinguished, you can cure your sacred tincture in a darker location. It can be hidden behind a cloth on your altar or in a cupboard.

13. Concentrate on your energy on all planes, body, mind, and spirit, as you shake the tincture. You can create your own chant to say as you shake your jar, but here is one example of what you might say every time you shake it: "With herbal infusions and magical concoctions, I shake your powers, releasing true. Giving strength, bringing light, magic set, in the correct tincture."

14. Shake the jar twice daily for at least a month, repeating your words and visualising your intentions as you do.

After a month, strain the liquid through cheesecloth to remove all of the herbal plant fibres. You can then dilute it with distilled water, bottle it, and store it for magical purposes!

Charge Your Bath with a Spell and Ritual

There are numerous herbs that can be used to create a ritual bath. The majority of the herbs you will use in your bath will most likely need to be contained in a sachet or a larger tea bag to avoid clogging your drain when you drain the bath. Additionally, you can add larger blossoms and petals to the water, creating a giant infusion to relax your body.

Ritual baths are incredibly healing for the body and spirit, and if you work with magic and herbal remedies, this spell will charge the herbs and charms used in your bath experience, ensuring that you are floating on the highest possible vibration of magic.

You'll require the following:
- A variety of herbs (depends on your spell work)
- Epsom or Sea Salt
- Herbal sachet
- Oils essentielles (optional)
- Bowl for mixing
- Candles (choose colours based on the requirements of your spell)

- Petals and heads of flowers (dry or fresh)
- Stick of smudge

Arrange your candles on your altar in a triangle or an arch. Make the farthest point of the triangle or arch from you. (Alternatively, if your altar is too small, you can perform this ritual on your kitchen table.)

1. Place the mixing bowl in the centre of your altar's candles.

2. Light each candle, invoking the candle magic energy that your spell requires. It is entirely up to you and your intentions, as well as the colour of the candle you have chosen.

3. Once the candles are lit, add your herbs one by one to the mixing bowl. Stir the mixture after each addition of a new herb. While bathing, you'll want to stir clockwise to add to or gain from your ritual bath, and counterclockwise to purify, remove, or release something. It is determined by your spell.

4. You may now add fresh or dried herbs, salt, magical powder, and essential oils, as well as anything else necessary for your spell, stirring in the appropriate direction with a sacred tool after each addition.

5. Once everything has been combined, light your smudge stick and allow it to smoke. Once the smoke begins to flow, swirl it into the mixing bowl in the direction you desire and say the following words: "Herbal mixture, green goddess light, enter my bath tonight." Purify after mixing with water. Lift my light, sacred magic."

Experiment with different words and phrases that pertain to your spell.

Additionally, you can bring your smudge stick into the bath later to smudge the water before entering.

1. Place your hands over the bowl of mixture and visualise the appropriate colour of light flowing through your hands and into the mixture. Any words that will invoke the energy required for your sacred bath ritual may be stated.

2. Once charged, begin filling the sachets with the herbal mixture, tying them off, and preparing them for the bath.

3. Remove the bowl from the altar and centre the sachets on the altar or workspace. You may leave them in place for as long as you believe they are necessary, or until the candles burn out.

4. At this point, your bath sachets are charged with your magic, and you may begin the ritual. While drawing your bath, stir the water in the same direction you stirred the herbs in the mixing bowl and incant some words to communicate your intentions and purpose to the water. While the water in the tub is spinning, add your sacred herbs to the water to steep.

5. Smudge the tub with some candles. You may smudge before or after drawing the bath; the choice is yours.

6. Infuse the bath with fresh or dried rose petals or other flower heads. Additionally, you can add a few drops of charged essential oils (you can perform the same candlelight work and visualisation charging on your essential oil bottles).

7. Allow the herbs to work their magic on your spirit while you soak in your bath.
   Visualize the effect you wish to invoke or manifest with this spell and allow yourself to be open to the possibilities.

8. As you drain the water, invite it to carry your magic into the universe and to manifest your intentions in life and all reality.

Spell of Herbal Love

Who doesn't want to have a little more love in their lives? Everyone desires a little love, and when you work with the energies and herbs that promote those relationships, emotions, and experiences, you give your love experience a significant boost.

With any spell, the devil is in the details and precisely what you are attempting to invoke or manifest. Love spells can be used to attract your true love, to arouse sexual passions, or to promote a stronger bond and marriage partnership.

Each spell requires your unique intentions and purposes, and as such, it is up to you to modify any ritual, potion, brew, or energy to match your desires.

It will be a simple energetic approach for this herbal love potion spell to allow for an increase in the power of love in your life. Whether to strengthen existing relationships or to attract new ones, this spell is designed to increase the passion and flow of love into your life.

You'll require the following:
- Roses
- Petals de rose
- Lavender
- Cinnamon
- Jasmine
- Peppermint

- Chamomile
- Rosemary

**

IMPORTANT NOTE: Herbs may be fresh or dried.
- Bowl for mixing
- Candles in pink and gold (3-5)
- Frankincense (cinnamon, jasmine, or rose)

This simple infusion is similar to making any other tea, but in order to charge and infuse it with your intentions, there are a few additional steps that will help you create a truly magical love potion. With the ingredients, you can be as creative as you want with the proportions.

Depending on your personality and personal preferences, you may prefer more jasmine than roses in your infusion. Due to the strong sedative properties of cinnamon and chamomile and lavender, you'll probably only need a pinch of each.

1. Begin this ritual the same way you did the previous one (see Spell and Ritual to Charge Your Bath), by arranging your candles in a triangle or arch on your altar or workspace, with the top or point furthest away from you.

2. Center your mixing bowl in the candle arrangement and light the candles with the following invocation: "Magic fire, candlelight, I invoke your strength and wisdom right now." Love is life, and mine is authentic; I choose to love and live it."

3. After lighting the candles, place your incense on the altar. You can make a statement at this time by burning aromatics to invoke the powers of love.

4. When ready to add the herbs, begin by adding them one by one.

In the light of love, communicate what each herb or flower means to you. Each one may have a unique essence and energy that is unique to you, and it is unique to everyone. Allow your intuition to guide your thoughts and words, and as you add each herb, speak the herb's magic.

5. Each time you add a new element to the bowl, stir it clockwise to increase the amount of love in your life and make it bigger.

6. Once all of your magical love herbs are combined in the bowl, infuse the love potion with your purpose and intentions.
You can empower your potion through creative visualisations, spoken words, and even by invoking Venus, the deity and goddess of love.

7. Allow the mixture to sit in the candlelight until the candle is completely consumed.
You may wish to relight some of your love incense to maintain the potency and aroma of the energy.

8. While you wait for the candle magic to charge your love potion, consume some love foods such as pomegranates, apples, figs, and berries. While eating these treats, visualise the love power you wish to invoke.

9. Once the candles have burned out, you can begin preparing a herbal infusion to drink. You might want to save some of your favourite foods to eat while sipping your tea.

10. Adjust the quantities to taste and add the love potion to boiling water, steeping for up to 10 minutes and no longer than 15 minutes before drinking.

11. Take pleasure in the warmth of a fire, the gentle light of the sun, or even the goddess moon.

12. You may also wish to incorporate these herbs into a sacred ritual love bath. To enhance your magical intentions, you can combine the sacred bath and the love potion infusion into one magical night of love power.

Ritual of Charging the Sun and Moon

Much of Wiccan practise is devoted to celebrating Mother Nature's cycles and rhythms, as well as the powerful energies associated with those cycles. Much of the magic work that you do has an intention-based energy that is connected to night and day, to the sun and moon's power.

Numerous spells and rituals are performed in conjunction with these significant cycles and energies, which can impart a powerful energetic charge on any spellwork or magical practise. The following ritual demonstrates how to charge your herbal potions, spells, and brews with the sun and/or moon's energy.

You'll require the following:

- Your choice of herbs (fresh or dry- depending on the spell)
- Mixing bowl made of glass, wood, or steel (alternative: sacred cloth for rituals)
- Stick of smudge
- Outside, a dry, secure location
- Moonlit evening
- A bright day

This ritual follows a similar pattern to others. You may wish to create an intention by casting a protective circle around your outdoor workspace or altar. Additionally, you can sprinkle a circle around your workspace with magical herbs and powders.

1. Bring all necessary ingredients outside to the area where you will be working.

2. Place the bowl there and light the candle and smudge stick if desired.

3. Smudge the area around your temporary outdoor altar space in a clockwise direction, as you will be charging your herbs or infusing them with sun or moon energy. This is an excellent time to scatter your magical or protective herbs throughout the space.

4. To the bowl or cloth, add the herbs of your choice, one at a time if using more than one, stirring clockwise with each addition. Additionally, you can burn your smudge stick at intervals while stirring. (If you are using a sacred cloth instead of a bowl for your herbs to lay out in the light, you can use your hand to spread the herbs around in a clockwise fashion, or sweeping motions)

5. As you add each herb, you can say some spell work words to invoke the herbs' energies and declare your intention to charge them with the light of the sun or moon (you can do an overnight into afternoon spell using both the sun and moon).

6. Once the herbs are combined, place your hands over them and visualise the silver light of moonlight or the golden light of sunlight entering them (or both, depending on your spell).

7. If you feel the need to cover the herbs to protect them from animals or rain, seek out a glass lid that allows light to pass through and avoid plastics if possible.

8. Continue to leave the herbs on the outdoor altar for as

long as you require moonlight, sunlight, or a combination of the two. Allow at least 5 hours and no more than 10, depending on the time of year and available daylight/moonlight hours.

9. Once you have finished with the charging ritual, you can close the circle, paying respects and gratitude to the sun and moon, and bring your herbal potion back inside to be jarred and stored.

10. If you feel the need to recharge the moonlight/sunlight charge on this jar of herbs, simply place it outside in a second ritual.

All of these rituals and spells are adaptable to your own practise and magical needs. All spells and rituals are forms of creative expression, so don't be afraid to think outside the box and peer through the kaleidoscope. There are a plethora of things you can do. Take pleasure in crafting your spells and rituals and watch your life transform in meaningful ways that contribute to the happiness, healing, and joy that come with a magical life!

Chapter 6
Wealth Spells

When witches cast wealth spells, they may not always be spells for money, as true wealth cannot always be quantified in monetary terms. And even if fortune favours you, what is the true cost?

Inquiring about wealth spells falls under the 'Be careful what you wish for' category. Is what you're doing truly in your best interests? You should consider these points carefully before casting wealth spells.

And always keep in mind: No Harm. Additionally, keep in mind that your wealth spell should be cast out of necessity, not greed. Request wealth only if you truly require it; otherwise, the magic will fail.

With that in mind, here are some effective simple wealth spells.

Prosperity Herbs
While you may believe that having a pot of herbs in your home has nothing to do with spells, consider the following. To begin,

you must learn which herbs possess magical properties and what they are, and then concentrate intently on the herb, believing it will bring you wealth. Therefore, keep a small pot of basil, parsley, rosemary, or thyme in your home to attract prosperity. Or multiples!

Change Bowl

Keep money in your pocket by keeping a bowl of change near the front door. To bring money into the home, add foreign coins and old, out-of-circulation coins.

Mandrake Currency

This one is for those who own retail businesses. Secure a large denomination note with an elastic band around a piece of mandrake root. Maintain it in your cash register and watch your revenue double. It will occur shortly.

Abundance Spell of the Candle

With this simple spell, you can use the energy and power of the candle flame to attract wealth to you. You will require:

- A green candle
- Cinnamon essential oil
- Vanilla essential oil
- A large denomination coin

With a sharp object – a craft knife, scalpel, or toothpick – carve the word 'Wealth' along the length of the candle. Now anoint the carved word with the oils. Place the coin in the candle holder, followed by the candle. Allow the candle to burn completely out.

When the candle burns out, take the wax-covered coin and store it safely to bring you wealth.

The Spell of Self-Love

This spell is centred on self-esteem and self-worth. It's very simple to do and only takes about ten minutes. It is the ideal spell, to begin with if you wish to pursue love spells further.

The following ingredients are required:
- One birthday candle (pink or red is preferable, but since this spell is specifically for you, use whatever candle speaks to you).
- Oils essentielles (orange, rose, jasmine, or sandalwood)
- One crystal of rose quartz
- A single piece of agate
- A pinch of pink Himalayan salt

Step 1: Using an upward stroke, anoint the birthday candle with the essential oil using a paintbrush.

Step 2: Melt the bottom of the candle with the lighter and then place it upright in the centre of your agate slice.

Step 3: Keep your rose quartz close to your candle to aid in promoting and enforcing your self-love intention.

Step 4: Begin by lighting the candle. To add an extra layer of protection, sprinkle the Himalayan pink salt in a circle around the candle.

Step 5: Sit in front of your burning candle and meditate. Consider all the aspects of yourself that you adore. With every fibre of your being, feel that self-love. If you find yourself reflecting on a negative situation that occurred, make an effort to transform it into a positive one. For instance, if you begin to recall an embarrassing statement you made to a coworker, attempt to flip it around by thinking: "Yes, that was embarrassing, but everyone makes embarrassing statements from time to time, and that is what makes us human." These emotions are natural, and I continue to love myself. Saying something embarrassing by accident does not make me any less loved or significant."

Step 6: As you meditate in silence, allow the candle to burn completely out. This process takes between ten and fifteen minutes. Allow yourself to be enveloped in positive emotions.
Spell of Invitation to Love

This spell will assist you in attracting love into your life and communicating to the universe that you are willing to love and be loved.

- Ingredients:
- Three candles in white
- Rosmarinus (a small piece is fine)
- One crystal of rose quartz
- Frankincense (vanilla preferably)
- A single small red box (a gift box is perfect)
- Felt-tip or pen in pink or red
- Essential oil of patchouli
- Three holders for candles
- An item that, in your opinion, embodies love

Step 1: Locate a location, either outdoors or indoors, where you feel secure and at ease. Ascertain that the area is relatively quiet so that you are not distracted. It's ideal to have a garden, forest, or even a favourite room in your home.

Step 2. Meditate for a few minutes to clear your mind of any distracting thoughts. When you are ready, use the patchouli oil to anoint all three candles.

Step 3: Arrange the candles in the candle holders directly on the floor or ground. It makes no difference which position you place them in. Begin chanting: "Love is present in my life and has found its way to me.
I have fallen in love, and they have fallen in love with me."

Step 4: Place the rose quartz in the box alongside the item you selected previously. You could even create a list of the characteristics you seek in a lover and use the list as your item. The box and its contents focus your intention and symbolise what love means to you.

Step 5: Take a hold of your box. Allow yourself to be overcome by feelings of love as you imagine what it will be like to finally possess the happiness that awaits you. Consider falling in love. Allow yourself time to reflect on these thoughts.

Step 6: Create a list of affirmations that relate to your desires. For instance, "I will be loved" is effective. Light your candles and repeatedly chant the affirmation you chose.

Step 7: Intentionally communicate your intentions to the universe by saying, "so be it." Snuff out your candles and then seal the box. Keep it closed until the love you requested enters your life. Following the fulfilment of your desires, you may remove the crystal and keep it nearby as a reminder of what the universe provided.

Spell of Fire Flowers
This spell is for those who have severed ties with a lover or even just a relationship that caused them distress and feel cut off from all forms of love in their lives. Additionally, it works for those seeking to clear the path to a brand-new relationship.

Ingredients:
- Graphite and Paper
- A cauldron or any other container that is not flammable
- One pink pillar candle
- A candle holder or a well-protected dish
- Three dried white flowers (for example, daisies, lilies, or daffodils)
- Frankincense (rose preferably)

Step 1: Locate a quiet, undisturbed location in which to perform this spell. Light the incense with a lighter or a match and allow the smoke to fill the area.

Step 2: Light the candle in its holder or on a safe dish.

Step 3: Gently remove one petal at a time from one of your chosen flowers. While doing so, chant the following words: "I am (inhale now) A powerful love (exhale) That burns like fire (inhale)"

Step 4: Begin removing the petals from the remaining two flowers, repeating the incantation for each flower. After that, place the petals in the cauldron or incense burner.

Step 5: Inhale slowly and deeply. Eliminate all distracting thoughts from your mind. When you are focused, write your full name on the piece of paper with the pencil.

Step 6: Using the candle's flame, start a fire in a corner of the paper.

Place the paper in the burner or cauldron and leave it alone to burn.

Allow the paper and candle to burn completely out at this point. When the paper has been reduced to ashes and the candle wick has been extinguished, bury the flower petals and ashes, preferably in a flowerpot or garden. Carry the candle in the same manner as the candle, but keep it separate from the other items.

Express gratitude to the universe and deities.

Bath for Attraction of Wealth

This bath cocktail can be used at any time, but it is most effective when used just before an important event that could result in financial gain. For instance, immediately prior to a business meeting, promotion, or financial opportunity. You will require the following:

- Several tablespoons sea salt
- 3 drops basil essential oil
- 3 drops cinnamon essential oil
- 3 drops pine essential oil
- A trace of dried patchouli
- A small bottle, such as a toiletries travel container

Fill your bath with hot water and add the oil and herbs. Soak for at least 15 minutes and visualise the outcomes you desire from the meeting or event, as well as the ways in which you wish it to bring you wealth. Fill the bottle and take it with you before draining the bathwater.

Spell of Abundance

This spell must be cast on a full moon night. Using a check from your chequebook, leave the date line blank. Write your full name on the payee line. Write 'Paid in Full' in the amount box and the same thing on the line where the words should be written.

Write 'Law of Abundance' on the signature line. Place the check in a secure location that is meaningful to you. You are not requesting anything specific; rather, you are requesting anything that may be due to you, which is why it works – 'need not greed.'

Spell of Lavender Money

A conjure bag, which is a red flannel bag used for magical purposes, is required for this spell. If you want to make one yourself, you can find instructions online or hire a witch to do so for you. However, the magic will almost certainly be stronger if you create your own.

After you've created your conjure bag, you'll need seven different denominations of money, depending on your home currency. Your money will increase sevenfold or even sevenfold.

Spell of Mint Prosperity

This spell must be cast within a sacred circle, which requires the presence of a mint plant and your wallet. Once the circle has been cast and the quarters have been called, take the mint to the Earth Quarter and use your hand to draw a pentagram over it. Reintroduce the mint to the altar and rub it along the edges of your wallet. Put a mint leaf in your wallet and carry it around to attract prosperity.

All of these spells are effective if you require wealth. It's entirely natural to desire wealth, and if you practise witchcraft, the next logical step is to believe you can cast a wealth spell. However, do you require that wealth, or is greed communicating that you do? If you are simply looking to increase your bank balance and are not in desperate need of additional funds, wealth spells will not work for you. You absolutely must comprehend this, as well as the fact that wealth is not always quantifiable in monetary terms.

Candle magic is perhaps the simplest form of spell casting, as it does not require an abundance of elaborate ritual or complex apparatuses. In a sense, anyone with a light can perform magic.

Consider the time you expressed a desire prior to blowing out the candles on your birthday cake. A similar thought applies to flame enchantment, except that rather than pursuing your desire for things to work out as expected, you're announcing it. Given the state of affairs, the birthday candle ritual is predicated on three critical supernatural standards:

Determine a goal.

Visualize the desired outcome.
Concentrate your intent, or will, on manifesting that outcome.
Candles come in a variety of shapes and sizes. There is a wide variety available at various occultist shops, body shops, and even grocery stores.

It is beneficial, however, to purchase from shops that specialise in magical intent, as this ensures that if you have any questions, you will speak with someone who is more likely to know what they are talking about than an average grocery store clerk.

While the majority of witches and those who practise magic rituals will tell you that the size of the candle is irrelevant, if the candle is excessively large and takes three days to burn out, you may not want to use it in a spell that requires the candle to burn completely out naturally, as most spells do. As a result, a large, bulky candle can actually be detrimental.

Tea lights, votive candles, tapers, columns, encased pillars, and free-standing pillars are the most common types of candles. While all of these types of candles are interchangeable, the best types for spells that require complete burning are votive and tapers. This is because their wicks are typically short, making them the most controllable. Menorah candles are one of the most popular candle types; they measure approximately four inches in length and are readily available in bulk at convenient locations such as the grocery store. They are white, thin, and unscented, making them ideal for the majority of spellwork.

In some instances, a spell or ritual may require a specific type of candle, such as one shaped like a particular figure to represent a particular person or a seven-day candle. The following is a brief list of the intentions behind a few commonly used candles in these instances.

This is used to attract or repel a specific individual, but it can also be used to represent someone close to you who identifies as female.

Male figure: This is used to attract or repel someone specific, but it can also be used to represent a close male relative.

Couple: Couple-shaped candles are used to bind a married couple together.

Genitalia: This one is fairly self-explanatory. It is used to stimulate sexual desire, arousal, and fertility.

Buddha: Prosperity, abundance, and good fortune

A devil-shaped candle is used to encourage or banish temptations.

The Cat: This is reserved for money spells, good fortune, and even protection.

Skull: This candle shape is used to ward off negative emotions and thoughts. Additionally, it is used in healing and cleansing spells.

The seven knobs that comprise the body of this candle symbolise seven wishes.

It is strongly recommended that you use a candle that has never been used in a spell. Do not simply take a candle that you burned for your nightly bath and use it in a money spell because you are out of money. If you are not in the mood to go out and purchase a new candle that day, you should postpone your spell work. According to the majority of magical beliefs, once lit, a candle absorbs the vibrations produced by the numerous items in its vicinity. This is believed to result in a negative or ineffective magical outcome, so caution is advised.

Colors and Their Meaning for a Wiccan

Colors serve a variety of functions in our world. They are used in art to convey a message or mood, to stimulate the mind through subtle or winding patterns, and even to organise. Colors are critical to a Wiccan's spell casting and intent. Each colour serves a purpose and has an intention in our daily lives. Certain days, emotions, and even numbers are associated with a particular colour.

Candles, with their extraordinary symbolic qualities, enable us to work directly with their magical properties. For hundreds of years, humans have associated various hues with distinct characteristics or events. For example, since red is the colour of blood and the heart, passion and love have always been associated with it.

Because the colour green is ubiquitous during the earth's growing season, it has long been associated with abundance and prosperity.

To cast the spells highlighted in this book accurately, you must carefully choose the colour of your candle and, ideally, perform the spells on a day of the week when the intent is clear. By incorporating these colour and time correspondences into your magic, you can reinforce the spell's intent and increase its potency.

Red is a colour that represents vitality, passion, strong emotions, fertility, desire, sexuality, and strength.

White: White symbolises purity, healing, the start of a new phase, the expulsion of evil spirits, peace, and innocence.

Pink is the colour associated with feelings of love, friendship, affection, reconciliation, and harmony.

Purple is symbolic of spirituality, wisdom, idealism, devotion, as well as spiritual strength, insight, and emotion.

Black: This colour is purifying. It symbolises security, stability, dignity, and the end (but also seed to a new beginning).

Blue: The colour blue is associated with healing, truth, wisdom, protection, the spirit, and patience.

Brown: Brown is a colour associated with solidarity, grounding, strength, endurance, and a sense of oneness with nature.

Yellow is the colour of joy, accomplishment, inspiration, knowledge, completion, and imagination.

Green: The colour green is associated with abundance, prosperity, growth, employment, balance, and renewal.

Gold symbolises integrity, inner strength, self-awareness, intuition, and comprehension.

Silver is the colour associated with intuition, vision, purity, healing, capability, memory, and intelligence.

Orange: This colour is associated with vitality, energy, communication, happiness, and attraction.

Grey: Grey is a colour associated with introspection, stability, reserve, and neutrality.

The Days of the Week's Intention

Monday is the moon's day, and it is associated with fertility, insight, wisdom, beauty, illusion, emotions, and dreams. Blue, white, and silver are the best colours to use on this day.

Tuesday is Mars's day and is associated with triumph, success, courage, defence, logic, vitality, and conviction. Today is an excellent day for problem-solving spells. On this day, the best colours to use are black, red, and orange.

Wednesday is ruled by Mercury and is associated with fortune, luck, change, creativity, education, insight, and self-improvement.

Orange, purple, and grey are the best colours to use on this day.

Thursday: Thursday is ruled by Jupiter and is associated with abundance, prosperity, healing, and protection. Purple, green, and blue are the best colours to wear on this day.

Friday is Venus's day, and it is associated with love, fertility, childbirth, romance, passion, friendship, and pregnancy. Green, pink, and blue are the best colours to wear on this day.

Saturday is ruled by Saturn and is associated with wisdom, transformation, purification, motivation, and spirituality. On this day, the best colours to wear are black, purple, and brown.

Sunday is ruled by the Sun and is associated with advancement, success, celebrity, prosperity, and wealth. Today is an excellent day to cast money spells. Gold, yellow, green, and orange are the best colours to use today.

After covering the days and colours, it's time to choose a candle. To choose the colour, it is best to align your intentions with the hue you choose and the day on which the spell is cast.

For instance, if you want to cast a wealth-multiplying spell, you should use a gold, yellow, or green candle and perform the ritual on a Sunday.

The effectiveness of your desired spell is entirely dependent on how you organise it. The closer the spell is cast to the intended day and in the appropriate colour, the more potent it will be. This is why it is critical to choose your candle with care and consideration.

Candle Magic Spell for Money Attraction

This spell is a simple and enjoyable way to attract more money into your life. It will combine several of the other magical items you've discovered and will require the use of a few additional items.

You'll require the following:
- 3 green enchantment candles with holders
- Combustible matches or a lighter
- Essential oil of vervain
- Mint leaves, crumbled
- Basil leaves, crumbled
- A rectangular piece of parchment paper
- A carving tool (a pin, a needle, or a knife) to carve a symbol into the wax
- Numerous coins of varying shapes, sizes, and origins

The Candle Magic Spell for Attracting Money: A Step-by-Step Guide

1. Draw a circle in the desired size.

2. Arrange your three green candles in an arc or semi-circle on the altar, with the top of the arc facing away from you.

3. Pick up a candle one at a time and perform the following:

Carve any prosperity symbols that you like or that are a part of your practise into the wax, anywhere on the candle and all over the candle (for inspiration, look at runes and Celtic symbols). Remove any wax that has naturally accumulated during the carving process.

Apply essential oil to the candle (you may use your own blend and have it diluted in carrier oil if desired).

Sprinkle the dried herbs evenly across the parchment paper.

Roll the anointed candle through the herbs and collect them around the candle's perimeter.

As you go through these steps for each candle, repeat the following phrase or something similar: "Candle magic was born with me; assist me in manifesting my destiny."

I pray for money, riches, and prosperity to come to me in good health.

This green candle will burn my truth, in order to attract abundance to me.

The powers that be will heed my appeal, which is simply to become richer now.

Thus it is"

4. After carving and anointing each candle, arrange them in their holders in a semi-circle and sprinkle the coins in front of them, saying the following words: "Money brought, and money sent, I ask for riches by divine rite lent."

I beg of thee, with open arms, to send me money three times three!

Thus shall it be!"

5. Light the candles and allow them to burn completely out to the end of the wick.

6. If you have any herbs left over from your candle rolling, you can now burn them as incense on top of a charcoal disc in your cauldron.

7. Draw a circle around the coins and bury them in the ground in your yard or garden.

While you can modify this money spell to your liking, you can get a better idea of how to incorporate candles into your rituals and spells by incorporating some other magical items and supplies.

Imbolc Candle Magic Spell

Imbolc is a time of year when we commemorate the Maiden's (Triple Goddess) birth and the arrival of Spring. It is a ritual that is traditionally observed with a large number of candles and the colour white. You may modify this spell as desired.

You'll require the following:

TEN WHITE MAGIC CANDLES + CANDLE HOLDER
If desired, jasmine essential oil + carrier oil (or a Spring blend of your choice)

Any type of white flower
Matches or a lighter incense of Hyacinth or a fragrance of early spring flowers

Candle Magic Spell for Imbolc:
1. Create your desired circle.

2. While contemplating the Maiden Goddess's magic, anoint each of your white candles with essential oil. You can even speak directly to her while consecrating your candles.

3. Place them in their holders and distribute them throughout your altar space. You may also place them in other areas surrounding the altar, as long as they are visible and safe.

4. Light your preferred incense and scatter the white flowers about.
Place a few flowers near or next to each of your candles to create a flower spray around each one.

5. If you have any leftover flowers, arrange them in any way that feels natural. You can also use flower petals instead of whole bouquets of flowers if that is easier or more affordable.

6. Begin lighting the candles and as you do, speak the following words, or something similar:
"Oh, Maiden Goddess of dazzling beauty,
Welcom te regresar de la noche del invierno.
I invite you now to join me here, surrounded by candlelight and flowers.
With all my heart and soul, I welcome thee, to bridge the divide between the dark and light worlds.

Spring has arrived.
Welcom, oh Maiden; may your abilities be used to the fullest!
Thus it is."

7. Indulge in some delectable foods, herbal teas, or other brews as you sit by the candlelight and toast the Maiden divine to the dawn of Spring.

With a little candle magic, any spell can be enhanced. Fire illuminates your cause and purpose and unites all of nature's elements into a single instrument of magic. Continue experimenting with various colours, crafts, and methods for creating magic with candles, and allow them to deliver your message to the Great Divine.

The majority of candle spells require the candle's flame to burn completely out naturally, without being disturbed. However, leaving a flame unattended, even if it is in the form of a candle, is rarely a good idea. Observing the candle burn down could take hours, depending on the type of candle used, and most people do not have the time. If you must leave your candle, simply place it in a safe location away from flammable objects. An empty tub or sink are both suitable locations to leave the candle while you go about your daily activities. Additionally, many oils used for anointing are highly flammable and must be handled with caution. Certain spells require that the candles be extinguished, and it's easy to forget that there is oil on one's fingers as they attempt to pinch the candle out. Extreme caution should be exercised when handling these oils.

As you explore and practise the magical properties of candles, you will quickly notice that if you take the necessary precautions and maintain your focus, along with a sincere intent to do no harm, your spell work will flourish with success.

Chapter 7
Circle-Casting

Circulating circles is a fundamental skill in witchcraft. It is frequently the first skill that beginners acquire. The concept of casting circles is somewhat complicated, even if the techniques are relatively straightforward.

Casting a circle, or circle-casting, is the practise of erecting a temporary space for the purpose of performing a ritual or performing magic. It is, by definition, circular. While Wiccans are the most common practitioners of circle-casting, Witches of other religions also cast circles. The circle is a makeshift temple, a place separate from the everyday world where you can work your magic.

Typically, the high priestess and/or priest will cast a circle at the start of a rite. Solitary practitioners are also capable of casting circles. The circle is released once the spell work is completed and the ritual is completed.

The circle is not a physical boundary, but a psychological one. It is not perceived or felt using your normal senses. A circle, on the other hand, can be detected energetically. Additionally, it is believed that this circle encompasses all worlds, not just our physical plane.

What Is the Purpose of Casting a Circle?
Numerous factors can obstruct your magic.

Chaos-feeding entities, people with opposing wills, and distractions from the outside world are just a few possible sources of interference.

Circulating in a circle is one way to help block out these influences and maintain focus. Due to the psychic vulnerability of a magical trance, many witches will cast a circle to help protect their minds.

The outer barrier is not the circle's only significant barrier. The internal barrier is equally critical. Magical energy frequently refracts and disperses throughout the Universe. The purpose of performing magic and rituals is to focus your energy on a specific goal. Having a circle enables you to gather and retain more energy. If you invoke specific deities or spirits, a circle provides them with a safe haven during your rite.

Thus, a circle is intended to keep disturbances out and energy in. While this is a simplification, it is a straightforward way to look at it. Additionally, it can be viewed as a means of enhancing the strength of your magic.

Is it Required for Me to Cast a Circle?
You are not required to make a circle. Not all traditions make use of a circle.

Without one, Egyptian, Norse, and other folk and shamanic magic practitioners operate freely. It is merely a useful technology, not an unbreakable rule.

How large and round should my circle be?

A Wiccan circle is traditionally nine feet in diameter. In Wicca, the number nine, or three times three, is extremely significant. They will have a ritual nine-foot cord in many traditions and in the majority of covens. They fold it in half and anchor it in the centre, then walk in a circle to trace the circumference of the circle.

That is not to say that you must have a nine-foot circle. This is merely an observation. You can customise your circle to fit the available space. However, you can make it too small.

To determine whether it is too small, gather your spell tools and yourself in the area you intended to use. If your circle is so small that you could accidentally penetrate its edges while gesticulating or reaching for something, it is too small. Now, if the circle is being cast for a coven, it should be large enough for everyone to maintain a comfortable level of separation from one another.

If, like the majority of solitary practitioners, you only have a bedroom or study in which to work your magic, a nine-foot circle is ruled out. A smaller circle is preferable to a larger circle that extends through furniture and walls. Generally, you don't want anything else in your circle except for yourself, your altar, and tools for spell work.

Circulation of Your Circle

It's always a good idea to check and double check that you have everything you need before casting your circle. Before you begin casting your circle, prepare your altar, bring your book of shadows, all of your spell and ritual tools, and anything else you may require in your space. The majority of people are averse to walking through their circle in order to obtain something once it has been cast. Having said that, if an emergency arises and you are required to leave immediately, do so.

Nothing catastrophic will occur if you leave your circle before it is closed. A child or pet may also walk through your circle without causing any disruptions.

Additionally, some people will draw a "door" if they need to exit their circle before their spellwork with a wand or athame is complete. Additionally, you can create the illusion of walking through a "curtain" there.

When you reenter your circle, simply walk around the circumference in a clockwise direction to reinforce it.

Before we get started with the circle casting methods, there are two terms you should familiarise yourself with that may appear in certain spells. Deosil is the first. Deosil translates as "clockwise." widdershins is the second. Widdershins is an antonym for clockwise.

Cast a Simple Circle

To begin, mark your circle. You must first determine the location of your circle. It doesn't matter if you're doing it in the space where your altar is, outside, or in your bedroom; you want to ensure that you're not disturbed.

While it is not required, some people choose to physically mark their circles with meaningful objects. To mark your circle, you can use a cord, crystals, or candles. Additionally, you can utilise crystals that correspond to the cardinal point.

Following that, you'll need to summon some energy that will protect and surround you and your work. Put yourself in the centre of your circle. Allow yourself to breathe deeply and relax. Consider how the crown of your head is beginning to open up like a funnel, allowing divine, white light to enter. This is the crown of your head, and it will always be connected to the Divine.

You can enlarge and amplify this at any time.

Extend your arms out in front of you, palms facing out. Each time you inhale, visualise yourself drawing all of that light into your crown, and each time you exhale, visualise yourself pushing the light out through your palms, enveloping you in a protective shield. As your space fills with this energy, you may experience a buzz or tingle, goosebumps, or an uplifted feeling.

Extend the arm with which you write out to the side and point to the outer edge of your circle. Spin three times counter-clockwise while mentally marking your circle with this divine light. Raise both hands above your head and pray: "I ask the God and Goddess to bless this circle, that I may be free and protected within it." Thus shall it be."

Your circle has now been formed; you may begin performing your ritual or casting spells. Simply spin counterclockwise to close this circle and feel the protective light dissipate.

Casting Advanced Circles

A compass and four candles are required. The four candles can be all white or they can be a mixture of blue, red, yellow, and green.

To begin, locate the four cardinal points using your compass. Each of these points should have a candle. If you have coloured candles, the green candle should face north, the yellow candle should face east, the red candle should face south, and the blue candle should face west.

Begin with the North candle, light it, and repeat: "Guardians of the North, Earth element, I invoke your presence during this ritual." Please join me in blessing this circle right now."

Transfer to the East candle, light it, and repeat: "Guardians of the East, element of Air, I invoke your presence during this ritual." Please join me in blessing this circle right now."

Continue to the South candle, light it, and repeat: "Guardians of the South, element of Fire, I invoke your presence during this ritual." Please join me in blessing this circle right now."

Transfer to the West candle, light it, and repeat: "Guardians of the West, element of Water, I invoke your presence during this ritual." Please join me in blessing this circle right now."

Point your wand or athame toward the outer edge of your circle. Three times in a clockwise direction, visualise a white light rushing into the crown of your head and being pushed out through your arm and tool to the circle's edge.

Take a seat in the circle's centre and allow your circle to be filled with divine light. "Please be present with me during this ritual, God and Goddess, guardian angels, and spiritual guides." Bless this circle and guard me. No unwelcome entities are permitted in this space; only pure, divine beings are permitted. This circle has been formed. Thus shall it be."

Now is the time to begin your ritual and spellwork. When closing the circle, be sure to blow out your candles in the reverse order in which they were lit and express gratitude to the elements for their presence.

Casting a Circle

This is a fairly straightforward circle casting, but you will require three, four, six, or nine instances of a particular object. You may choose any number and any item that resonates with you, but they should all be similar objects. For instance, you could incorporate four houseplants, nine candles, three rocks, or six seashells into your arrangement. You are welcome to use any sacred items you possess.

To begin casting your circle, hold your objects in your hands and create an intention for them as you move around it, placing them to mark the circle's edge. If you are using candles, you will want to ensure that they are placed safely so that they can be lit safely without igniting anything.

If you feel compelled to say something as you do this, you may do so now; however, this circle casting does not require it. After you've placed all of your items, you can begin working on your spell or ritual.

To complete this circle, simply pick up your items in the opposite direction they were placed.

Circulating Within Your Circle

Once all of the work is completed, you must close your circle. When you release your circle, the energies contained within have a chance to dissipate and the space has a chance to revert to its pre-ritual state.

You can close your circle in a variety of ways, including by ringing a bell, performing the casting in reverse, or visualising the walls dissolving.

Gathering your tools and storing them will also assist in

dispersing the energy.

If you forget to close your circle, or if you close it improperly, the circle will fade away on its own after a few minutes or hours. If you use that area regularly for ritual work, it may help to slow the dissipation. That is not to say you should make it a habit of simply walking away. Always keep your circle closed.

Chapter 8
Dreams and Meditation

Meditation is scientifically proven to be beneficial to everyone. It connects you on all levels to your mind, body, and spirit, assisting you in attaining a higher state of awareness while also promoting physical health. Meditation is frequently associated with spirituality and its numerous practises, and while you might not expect it to be incorporated into Wiccan practise, it is one of the primary attributes.

Almost every spell and ritual I perform includes a meditation period. I must meditate in order to establish a connection with my inner knowing and the divine source energy with which I am working. It takes only a few moments and brings me closer to the energy of all things, bringing me into ultimate balance.

Meditation is not something you must learn; it comes naturally as you work with your Magic, and if you are simply open to being with yourself and your Magic, you are in meditation.

In general, meditation is a natural part of communing with

one's own soul and the soulful energy that pervades everything in life.

The purpose of studying witchcraft is to improve one's life. This is possible through the use of magic. You may find yourself completely immersed in a new, more adventurous way of life. Using magic to improve your life requires a great deal of practise.

Magic is not something that most people are naturally gifted with. To accomplish anything, you must first get out of your head. The Wiccan culture places a premium on life enhancement, which is why it attracts so many people.

Despite the fact that many people are drawn to this religion, many people leave it as well, and this is because they are unwilling to put in the effort necessary to improve their lives.

They anticipate that they will only need to say a few phrases and the magic will occur. This is partly due to the way magic is portrayed in the media. Consider the hit television series Charmed. It depicts three witches battling evil using only a few simple spells, which is not true. The same is true of the majority of available literature. Wiccans are frequently portrayed as people who congregate in the woods, recite a few spells, wave a few herb sticks, and presto—magic. It is more difficult than these portrayals suggest.

Spells require practise and must be performed multiple times to achieve mastery. Additionally, there are several distinct components to spells that you must master; once mastered, you can advance to the next level and practise those spells for hours on end without seeing any results. To develop into a powerful witch, you must devote a great deal of time and effort to your craft. The cost of being slothful will keep you at the same level for an eternity.

You cannot anticipate that life enhancement will transform your life into one of leisure.

This is another reason for people to abandon Wicca. They anticipate being able to make their crush fall in love with them and using magic to become wealthy, which simply does not happen—at least not immediately.

These things require effort and commitment.

Individuals have also joined and then abandoned the movement by becoming black witches. They discovered ways to amass wealth and coerce someone into falling in love with them. However, that magic comes at a cost, and that cost is not insignificant.

These individuals will literally sell their souls to a demon in order to obtain their desired outcome. You want to avoid these witches. If a person dies at the hands of a black witch, their soul is tortured for all eternity.

You will not be reincarnated; instead, you will be directed to purgatory.

Purgatory is the afterlife destination for the spirits of those who have committed evil deeds and used black magic. This is not the desired outcome. Every day, your spirit will be torn apart until the end of time, and despite the fact that your body will be dead, you will still be able to feel it because you are your spirit. Allow those who join Wicca and convert to the black witches' parish to do so of their own volition.

In any case, how do you use magic to improve your life? You have a connection to the earth. You establish relationships with others. You surround yourself with things that will enrich and delight you. These things are possible through the use of magic. It may appear that magic cannot accomplish anything that you cannot accomplish on your own, and this may be true to some extent.

However, as a member of the Wiccan religion, it is significantly easier to perform these tasks using magic than it is without magic.

Here are some ways that magic can help you improve your life:

Developing Friendships - Friendships are scarce, and even if you have a large group of them, they may not be the best kind.

As humans, we are drawn to what are referred to as "shiny people."

These are typically the people who are enjoyable to be around. However, these gleaming individuals are generally not the best company, as they appear to hang around only if you can do something for them.

Humans are also easily swayed by dramatic individuals. These are the people who are constantly loud and doing things they shouldn't be doing. It's exciting and enjoyable. However, if they turn on you, the experience can be unpleasant. These people can be toxic, and toxicity is the best way to ruin a friendship.

You want to hang onto these people because you think that they bring a lot of joy to your life, but the truth is they are only dragging you down. Usually, people feel obligated at the requests of shiny people—starting to ring any bells? To spot a toxic friend all you should do is try to do something that you want to do for yourself or ask for a favour, and watch them try to drag you down or not participate.

This is where magic comes in. Magic will draw in the right type of friends so that you can make a lasting bond with them, and not have to worry about them walking out of your life because you reach a milestone in your life, and can't take them to the mall twenty times a week anymore. Instead, these friends will root for you, encourage you to be the best that you can be, and they will not bat an eye when you do something to improve your life.

Magic will help you find the love of your life and someone who will bring you soup when you are sick. You'll attract the type of person who doesn't care whether you're wearing your pyjamas all day or a $300 gown when they see you. These friends are scarce, and magic will bring them into your life. This way, you can be certain that you are associating with the right people.

Assist You in Finding True Love - True love is the most difficult to come by. You may fall in love several times throughout your life and may even marry, but the likelihood is that it is not everlasting love. Love is everywhere, and it can be quite easy to find at times.

True love, on the other hand, is difficult to find because people are looking for the wrong identifiers. They want excitement and butterflies in perpetuity, and while those are fine to have with your partner in twenty years, the butterflies will eventually fade or will occur less frequently. When that occurs, you want to be able to wake up and greet the person beside you with a good morning kiss while still feeling good about it. How are you going to love them for the rest of your life if you don't?

Find someone who gives you a warm feeling in your heart and makes you happy even when the butterflies fade. True love is the kind of love that allows you to argue all day and then laugh and be happy for months at a time. True love is waking up next to the one you love and witnessing them in their most vulnerable state, which makes you love them even more.

This is the love that people seek incessantly, and it is a love that few people find. Some are duped into believing they discovered it because the butterflies last longer than usual, then marry and divorce five years later. This is because they have recently discovered someone they have lusted after for a longer period of time than usual.

Enter the realm of magic. Magic will bring you someone who can make your heart race while simultaneously making you feel calm. It will connect you with the person who will hold your hair while you are ill and rub your sore feet. It will provide you with someone who will assist you with the dishes for the remainder of your years. Someone who wakes up with you at 2:00 a.m. to bake cookies when you're unable to sleep.

You want to be around someone who supports the Wiccan religion so that you can be yourself. Once you let go and allow fate to show you who you should truly be with, these spells will assist you in strengthening your relationships while also assisting you in forming a bond with someone to create an unbreakable relationship.

Allowing fate to take control is the most difficult part. You want to meet someone you like, but the majority of people do not trust fate to choose someone for them because they already have someone in mind to be their forever love.

They are averse to relinquishing control for fear of something vanishing.

Are you going to fall in love with someone who is truly the

one for you, or are you going to spend the rest of your life fighting with the person you married and attempting to repair your relationship with countless spells? The choice is entirely up to you, but with a little patience and time, you will discover the person you have been waiting for.

Bravery - If you are not particularly courageous in any aspect of your life, have no fear. You are not alone in this. The average person lacks courage in at least one area of their life. This can include conversing with strangers or attempting to climb the corporate ladder. There are numerous aspects of life that require courage; it is impossible to be courageous in every one of them.

For instance, you may be able to skydive, but the prospect of speaking with that stunning person who has caught your eye terrifies you completely. And that's fine; you can't be courageous in every situation. Or perhaps you excel at interpersonal communication and public speaking but are terrified of riding an elevator.

There are numerous fears, and you cannot overcome them without courage. Many people overlook magic's ability to increase one's courage levels. Courage is critical, and spells can help you become a little bit stronger. As a witch, this is one of the most vital abilities you can have because you will have to confront people.

Whether it's defending an ancient tree against a company that wants to destroy it or preventing a black witch from ruining someone's life, many actions require courage.

Magic can assist, and it can provide far more than a smidgeon of courage. Magic can make you feel as if you are capable of conquering the world.

You will feel as though you can accomplish anything, which is exactly what you want. Bear in mind that the effects are not permanent and that you may need to reapply the spell several times.

After a few times of experiencing how great it feels to stand up to something that terrifies you, you will no longer require the spell because you will be able to be courageous on your own.

Good fortune - Luck is difficult to come by, and many people are in desperate need of it. You need luck to play the lottery, and you also need luck to ask the love of your life to marry you, which is something that not many people consider. As with courage, luck is a necessary component of survival in life. It is not always necessary to rely on hard work, as hard work can only take you so far. As an example, consider working in a large law firm where you and the partner's pet are competing for a promotion.

You may perform the more difficult tasks and work the hardest, but they have an advantage over you due to their status as a favourite. In this case, a little good fortune may be beneficial. Rather than having a clear winner selected before the race even begins, luck can ensure that they are paying attention to your efforts.

You can create talismans and good luck charms using a few simple spells, or simply cover yourself in an aura of good luck using some spells; these spells are generally not difficult. However, the more luck you desire, the stronger the witch you must be, as a stronger witch casts a stronger spell. Additionally, when you are more powerful, you are required to "reapply" less frequently. Additionally, a reason to practise, correct? Everyone wishes to be fortunate, so make an effort to develop into the best witch you can be.

A job interview is an example of a real-world scenario. You want to use these spells liberally, because the more luck you have, the more prepared you will be for an interview, and the easier it will be to land the job. Avoid becoming arrogant; even if you apply and interview, if you are not a good fit, no matter how much magic you use, you may not get the job.

Bear in mind that there is a significant difference between confidence and arrogance. Confidence is knowing that you are capable of doing the job. Being cocky is believing that you can do something better than everyone else without any training. Cocky believes you are a shoe-in for a job you have never held. Confidence is knowing that you are a quick learner who will perform well on the job even without training. You want to project confidence while remaining humble. Recognize that you are not the ideal candidate, but also that you are the best candidate.

Mental Clarity - Have you ever had a burning question in your mind or been forced to make a difficult decision? Is it true that it took you longer than you care to admit to accomplishing your objectives with these scenarios?

That is something that everyone experiences at some point in their lives, and it is perfectly normal. You want to have a clear mind, which is more difficult to achieve than you might believe. And, even if you clear your mind, it's frequently difficult to come up with a clear answer. You search and search, but everything has advantages and disadvantages.

This makes it difficult to find time to do what you want to do when you want to do it, as you are still agonising over the decision or attempting to sort everything out—decisions can be messy.

If you're having difficulty deciding where to go in life, you can use a spell to assist you. There are numerous spells that assist you in opening your mind to make the correct choice, and much of it involves Divination. Yes, prophesying enables you to make the best choices possible by providing insight into the outcome of your choices. There are spells available to help you clear your mind, and there are spells available to help you obtain the answers you seek.

These are the spells you want to use to navigate life and truly make the right choices. Perhaps you're wondering if your spouse is being unfaithful and are unsure whether you should pursue the matter. Cast a spell to obtain the information you seek. Feel no remorse if they are not cheating. You are not considering their personal consequences; rather, you are conducting research prior to confronting them, as a rational person would.

Putting an End to Evil - Let's face it, we are frequently surrounded by evil. Without a doubt, this world is a demonic playground. It is becoming more difficult to find a pure environment in these times, and those who are good are frequently attacked by the world.

Have you ever felt as if the entire world was conspiring against you, and despite the fact that the evil people appear to live happy lives, you are miserable?

That is what many people face when attempting to live decent lives, as it appears as though life despises goodness and rewards evil. There are ways to maintain your purity and that of your environment. Have a suitable location in which to work your magic. You want your mind to be pure and free of other, evil witches' attacks as well.

There are numerous spells available for purifying not only the area, but also the mind. Smudging is one of the most common types of purification spells.

If you practise frequently, you should probably smudge your area before each spell; however, if you practise infrequently, once a week or biweekly should suffice. Simply ensure that you cleanse it prior to performing a spell. The more pure your spells are, the more effect they will have on your life, and evil forces will be unable to counteract them.

There are several other spells that you can use to ensure that your mind and environment remain free of evil.

Candles are required for this (white candles especially). They provide you with pure energy with which to cast your spells. White candles act as a direct conduit to the Goddess, assisting you in preventing other entities from responding to your calls. Although the majority of spells do not require white candles, it is always a good idea to light one whenever you perform a spell.

Healing - As a beginner in Wicca, you can alleviate side effects and a variety of other issues that exist beneath and on top of the surface of one's skin. You can assist with mental illnesses.

While these diseases cannot be cured, you can help alleviate symptoms such as depression and anxiety.

Additionally, you can assist someone who suffers from PTSD in sleeping better at night.

When magic is used to benefit others, including yourself, it is wonderful. Additionally, unlike with pain and suffering from a major physical injury, it does not require a great deal of magical strength to assist in alleviating the symptoms of illnesses.

- Prosperity Have you ever been unemployed and had to look for any source of income to keep the lights on? It's not enjoyable, and it's becoming increasingly difficult to find jobs that pay the bills and keep food on the table. That is the disadvantage of the world in which we live. Electronic and outsourced jobs are becoming more prevalent. And, unfortunately, unless you live in a commune, you cannot survive without money.

There are numerous spells available to assist you in gaining the upper hand with prosperity. It's a good idea to collect a large number of them so that you can douse yourself in luck and prosperity if you ever find yourself in need of it. Likewise, for healing spells.

Become a Master of Meditation

The best way to understand meditation is as a period of silence during which you can listen to your higher self. Meditation aids in concentration and focusing attention on the higher level of consciousness that exists within each of us. A daily meditation session can help clear the mind of clutter and maintain an open channel of communication.

A Guide to Meditation

Meditation is best described as 'listening.' It is the ability to hear one's Higher Self or Inner Self. According to some, it's like hearing the gods or the creative force. Simply put, the Higher Consciousness is listening. All of these are possible forms of meditation.

When meditation is used properly, it results in personal advancement.

Meditation is the simplest technique for spiritual advancement and can be practised in a group or alone.

Meditation is a practise that calms the conscious mind, the mind that is concerned with daily activities and life as we know it, and allows you to connect with your higher consciousness, also known as the subconscious, the part of your mind that is responsible for involuntary bodily functions, reflex actions, and what you might refer to as 'Universal Memory.'

Meditation's Dynamic

To fully comprehend the dynamics of meditation, one must first understand the nature of human consciousness and the fact that humans are both physical and spiritual beings.

These two facets of human nature are connected at the vital centres, which are referred to as Chakras in Sanskrit. Psychic energy travels through these chakras during meditation. The kundalini force is a powerful force known as the 'Serpent Power,' and once it flows through you, your chakras begin to open sequentially.

Meditation Mastery

If you approach the art with the incorrect technique, or even if you approach it without any technique, you may experience failure in meditation. Concentrating on your 'third eye,' the area one inch above your brow line and one inch inward from your forehead, is believed to focus energy in your crown chakra. The direction in which you focus your eyes also plays a significant role in the Third Eye meditation technique. Turning your gaze upward has to do with the energy in your higher consciousness and spiritual energy. Straightening your eyes outward expresses your conscious mind, whereas focusing downward expresses your subconscious mind.

When performing meditation, it is best to choose a position. Although meditation is traditionally performed in the lotus position, this position is not always comfortable, and it is preferable to be in a position of your own choice.

You may sit on the floor, in a chair, or on your back as long as your spine is straight.

The more at ease you are, the more energy and mental focus you have. When choosing a location for your meditation, it is critical that the space is quiet; naturally, your cleaned and censored circle is the best choice.

However, if you choose another space for whatever reason, it is best to clean it up and censor it similarly to how you did with your Circle. While facing a specific direction during meditation is not required, facing east is occasionally suggested.

However, your comfort is paramount, and so if you have a better view in another direction, do not hesitate to confront it! You are also free to choose the time of day you meditate, as well as the position, direction, and space in which you meditate. However, it is best to meditate at the same time each day to ensure consistency. Thus, the most convenient time is one that is quiet and peaceful but still manageable on a daily basis.

It must be done consistently in order to maintain success and success in meditation. Some recommend fifteen to twenty minutes of meditation twice a day. At the very least, you can get by with a single fifteen-minute session per day.

Again, consistency is critical— it's critical to adhere to the scheduled number of sessions as well as the times.

How to Congregate for a Wiccan Meditation

Wicca is truly a modern religion steeped in ancient witchcraft traditions. While drawing from the moon and invocation of the goddess are identical to mediation, daily meditation can help you deepen your Wicca practise and promote peace with the divine.

Assign your mind to a state of deep meditation.

Candles, incense, and singing all contribute to a relaxing state of relaxation. You can either listen to a singing CD or sing the name of a deity or goddess that you admire. Reduce the brightness of the lights or turn them off entirely.

Choose a place of relaxation that speaks to you.

Additionally, if you practise Celtic Wicca, you should practise counselling outside. Your passion for the sights, smells, and sounds of nature serves as your meditation. The majority of Wiccans prefer to meditate on their altars, particularly in inclement weather. The trick is to choose a meditation location that naturally makes you feel relaxed. As you mediate indoors, ensure that the room is silent and undisturbed.

Locate a convenient location.

It makes no difference whether you sit, lie down, or walk as long as you are comfortable and relaxed. Your objective is to remain alert and receptive, so avoid falling asleep too easily.

Determine the type of mediation you will conduct.

Passive meditation is a technique for allowing images to arise in your mind and focusing on them. With open or closed eyes, you should meditate consciously on the image or symbol on which you wish to focus. If you allow a symbol to enter you or if you choose one, send the image you've chosen. Among the subjects to be considered are the following: /magic God/Daughter Magic(ies)

Tree(s), flower(s), or plant(s) Gemstones (crystal, amethyst, sapphire, etc.

Shut your eyes. Shut your eyes. Concentrate on your intake for a few minutes.

Observe your own breathing. If your breathing is slow and steady, bring your sensing to your feet and shift your focus all the way up to your body. Eliminate any tension you may be experiencing in your body. Additionally, you can pause and reflect on stress, wondering why there is pressure.

Consider the positive energy that pervades your life.

Inhale deeply and visualise your feet glowing with white light all the way to the top of your head. Exhale the white light and allow it to float freely into your enchanted space.

Allow thoughts to arise during passive meditation.

If a thought or image fascinates you, begin focusing on it, then let it go and allow the next thought to surface. When practising active meditation, close your eyes and direct your attention to the symbol or image you've chosen. (If your thoughts begin to wander, bring your attention back to your breathing and begin again.) You may prefer to keep your eyes open and concentrate on your preferred symbol. Give it your all and consider all of its facets.

Keep a notebook and pen on hand in the area.

Perhaps you'd like to jot down ideas or draw pictures while you meditate. After that, return to your meditative state.

Thank you for your time.

Conclusion

Wicca is a highly effective way of life. It is a fundamental reality that has the potential to bring you so much inner peace, abundance, fertility, and prosperity on all levels of your life. You can be grateful for your life because we are all here to live and seek our truth alongside the Great Mother and Father Sky, held by the universe as we explore our eternal destinies and practise knowing who we are from deep within the blanket of Magical truth.

I am here to instil faith in you and educate you about the Wiccan path so that you can advance your own Magic and self-discovery. I hope you found the information you were looking for to inspire a more in-depth existence within the craft you are developing in your life.

Allow these concepts, teachings, guidelines, and tutorials to instil in you the confidence necessary to sustain your own fully alive and awakened Wiccan practise. Your true power is within you, and worshipping the divine in all things is the essence of wholeness in your life and in yourself.

Continue to educate yourself on new concepts, histories, methodologies, and transformations as you progress along your journey to help you develop your practise into the work of art it is destined to be. Allow your intuition to guide you and provide you with the courage necessary to fulfil your Magical dreams.

Everything you do from now on will be a gift to yourself in terms of spells, rituals, altar space, Book of Shadows, and daily practises. This way of life is abundant and there are numerous ways to enjoy it. The second major takeaway from this book is that you can be truly crafty and creative with your work and inner world in order to bring more harmony into your life.

The final takeaway is that Wicca connects you divinely to all of the universe's energies. It demonstrates that we all contribute significantly to the energy of all creation and that by performing rituals and spells, you are declaring that you are present and available to live your life through Magic and awareness of all that is around you.

9 783986 539061